Contemplation and Action

Naṣīr al-Dīn Ṭūsī

CONTEMPLATION AND ACTION

The Spiritual Autobiography of a Muslim Scholar

A New Edition and English Translation of

Sayr wa Sulūk

by

S. J. Badakhchani

I.B.Tauris
LONDON • NEW YORK
in association with
The Institute of Ismaili Studies
LONDON

Published in 1998 by
I.B.Tauris & Co Ltd
Victoria House
Bloomsbury Square
London WC1B 4DZ

175 Fifth Avenue
New York NY 10010

in association with
The Institute of Ismaili Studies
42–44 Grosvenor Gardens
London SW1W 0EB

In the United States of America
and in Canada distributed by
St Martin's Press
175 Fifth Avenue
New York NY 10010

A full CIP record for this book is available from the British Library
A full CIP record for this book is available from the Library of Congress

ISBN 1 85043 908 7

Library of Congress catalog card number: available

Typeset in ITC New Baskerville by Hepton Books, Oxford
Persian text typeset by HKH Design, London
Printed and bound in Great Britain by WBC Ltd, Bridgend

The Institute of Ismaili Studies

The Institute of Ismaili Studies was established in 1977 with the object of promoting scholarship and learning on Islam, in the historical as well as contemporary contexts, and a better understanding of its relationship with other societies and faiths.

The Institute's programmes encourage a perspective which is not confined to the theological and religious heritage of Islam, but seek to explore the relationship of religious ideas to broader dimensions of society and culture. They thus encourage an interdisciplinary approach to the materials of Islamic history and thought. Particular attention is also given to issues of modernity that arise as Muslims seek to relate their heritage to the contemporary situation.

Within the Islamic tradition, the Institute's programmes seek to promote research on those areas which have, to date, received relatively little attention from scholars. These include the intellectual and literary expressions of Shiʿism in general, and Ismailism in particular.

In the context of Islamic societies, the Institute's programmes are informed by the full range and diversity of cultures in which Islam is practised today, from the Middle East, Southern and Central Asia and Africa to the industrialized societies of the West, thus taking into consideration the variety of contexts which shape the ideals, beliefs and practices of the faith.

The publications of the Institute fall into several distinct categories:

1. Occasional papers or essays addressing broad themes of the relationship between religion and society in the historical

as well as modern contexts, with special reference to Islam, but encompassing, where appropriate, other faiths and cultures.
2. Proceedings of conferences or symposia.
3. Works exploring a specific theme or aspect of Islamic faith or culture, or the contribution of an individual figure or writer.
4. Translations of poetic or literary texts.
5. Editions or translations of significant texts of a primary or secondary nature.
6. Ismaili studies.

This publication comes under category five.

In facilitating these and other publications, the Institute's sole aim is to encourage original, interesting and mature thought, scholarship and analysis of the relevant issues. There will naturally be a diversity of views, ideas and interpretations, and the opinions expressed, will be those of the authors.

Contents

Acknowledgements

The publication of the present edition and English translation of the *Sayr wa sulūk* has been made possible by the support and assistance of a number of people, among them Professor Muhsin Mahdi of Harvard University who first urged me to undertake this task, and Professor Herman Landolt of McGill University who contributed to the preparation of the initial draft of the translation.

In the course of finalizing the text for publication, I received invaluable help from the late John Cooper when we were both graduate students at the Oriental Institute in Oxford. Subsequently he was appointed E. G. Browne Lecturer in Persian Studies at the University of Cambridge and also taught in the Graduate Programme in Islamic Studies and the Humanities at The Institute of Ismaili Studies, London. John Copper's scholarship was exceptional and his willingness to share it exemplary. His death shortly before the publication of this book has removed from our midst a most promising scholar of Islamic Studies in general and of Shi'ism in particular.

I am also much indebted to Professor Wilferd Madelung who kindly looked at the translation on more than one occasion and to Farhad Daftary for his unfailing encouragement and enthusiasm.

I would further like to record my gratitude to my colleagues at The Institute of Ismaili Studies who have facilitated this publication in various ways, in particular Kutub Kassam for his editorial expertise in the English part of the work, Faquir M. Hunzai who, apart from proofreading the Persian text, made a number of useful suggestions on the translation; and Alnoor Merchant of the Institute's library.

My words of thanks cannot be complete if I do not mention

the support and inspiration that I have received from my wife, Pari Badakhchani, without whom this work might not have materialized.

Finally, while I am greatly indebted to all those I have mentioned for making this publication possible, any errors or shortcomings in it are entirely my own responsibility.

S.J.B.

Note on the Text

The *Sayr wa sulūk* was not traditionally listed in the inventory of Ṭūsī's writings; but on the basis of its style, content and autobiographical evidence, contemporary bibliographers have now come to accept that it does come from the pen of Ṭūsī. This recognition first emerged after the publication in 1956 of an abridged version of the text, called *Guftārī az Khwāja-yi Ṭūsī bi rawish-i Bāṭinīyān*, by the Iranian scholar Muḥammd Taqī Dānish-pazhūh. Simultaneously, to commemorate the 700th anniversary of Ṭūsī's death, a collection of his Persian treatises was published by Muḥammad Taqī Mudarris Raḍawī under the title of *Majmū'a-yi rasā'il*. This collection included the text of *Sayr wa sulūk* which was, in fact, the complete version of the *Guftār*.

Mudarris Raḍawī's edition was based mainly on two relatively modern manuscripts: a copy at Dānishkada-yi Adabiyyāt Library (Qazwīnī collection), with corrections and marginal notes by two eminent Iranian scholars, namely Sayyid Naṣr Allāh Taqawī (editor of Nāṣir Khusraw's *Diwan*), and Muḥammad Qazwīnī (editor of Juwaynī's *Tārīkh-i jahān-gushāy*); and a copy that Mudarris Raḍawī had prepared for himself from an earlier printed version of the text based on older manuscripts. In the notes to his edition, Mudarris Raḍawī also speaks of several other printed versions of the *Sayr wa sulūk* known to him.

It is very likely that all these texts, including the ones used by Mudarris Raḍawī, were based on one or more of the following manuscripts: (i) Majlis Library, no. 5138/61, dated 1024–1057/1615–1647, and no. 5063/2, dated 1328/1910, which was prepared for Naṣr Allāh Taqawī and collated with other manuscripts; (ii) Dānishgāh Tehran, no. 1079/5, dated

1047/1637; (iii) Danishkada-yi Ḥuqūq Library, text of the *Guftārī az Khwāja*, no. 62/19, no date; (iv) Aṣghar-i Mahdawī, no. 364/37, dated 1240/1824; (v) Malik Library, no. 6193/8, dated 1279/1862; (vi) Āstān Quds, Mashhad, ms. no. 12243/10, copied by Asad Allāh Munajjim Dudānga Hizār Jarībī, dated 1306/1888.

The present edition of the *Sayr wa sulūk* is an improved version of the text, which was arrived at by collating Mudarris Raḍawī's edition with the *Guftār*, as well as other works of Ṭūsī, in particular the *Rawḍa-yi taslīm*, *Āghāz wa anjām*, *Tawallā wa tabarrā* and *Maṭlūb al-mu'minīn*, in which some of the topics discussed in this work occur frequently, sometimes in more or less identical language.

In this edition, apart from applying contemporary Persian orthographical conventions, I have corrected the typographical errors and in two instances reconstructed the text as indicated between square brackets.

The system of transliteration adopted for Persian and Arabic scripts is a modified version of the one used in the new edition of the *Encyclopaedia of Islam*, except for the letters dj, k and č which have been replaced by j, q and ch; and the ligatures have been dispensed with.

As for the translation, in most cases wherever a technical term has been used in English, its transliterated form is italicized in parenthesis, but in the case of some key words like *ta'līm* which recur frequently, I have preferred to retain them untranslated. Some Arabic and Persian words which have found their way into English dictionaries, such as 'Imam', 'Ismaili', 'Shi'i' and 'Sunni', have not been transliterated. Occasionally, I have added a word or a phrase to the translation within square brackets in order to render a more coherent translation.

As a general rule, dates are given according to both the lunar Islamic and Christian calendars. In the notes and bibliography, some of the publication dates are also given according to the solar Islamic calender used in Iran; these are marked 's' for *shamsī* (solar).

In both the Persian and English texts, passages that deal

with a significant idea or with a cluster of related ideas are numbered [§] to facilitate cross-reference between text, translation and introduction.

It should be noted further that references to the Qur'ānic verses cited by the author are given only in the English version and follow the numbering system of Yūsuf 'Alī's edition; for the interpretation of these verses, however, I have consulted a number of modern English translations.

Introduction

Naṣīr al-Dīn Ṭūsī and the Ismailis

Naṣīr al-Dīn Abū Ja'far Muḥammad b. Muḥammad b. Ḥasan al-Ṭūsī, the renowned Persian astronomer, philosopher and theologian, often referred to in general Shi'i literature as *muḥaqqiq-i Ṭūsī* (the great scholar Ṭūsī) and in the Ismaili circles of his time as *sulṭān al-du'āt* (king of the *dā'īs*),[1] was born in Ṭūs, which is now a small town in the suburbs of Mashhad, Khurāsān, on 11 Jumādā I 597/17 February 1201, and died in Baghdād on 18 Dhu'l-Ḥijja 672/25 June 1274.

Not much is known about Ṭūsī's childhood and youth other than what we find in the present autobiographical work, the *Sayr wa sulūk*. In this account Ṭūsī tells us that he was born in a family who followed 'the exoteric aspects of the *sharī'at*'[2] and whose profession was 'to promulgate the exoteric sciences,' which means that they were probably associated with the Twelver Shi'i clergy. It has been suggested, though without convincing evidence, that Ṭūsī was born in an Ismaili family and received his early education in Twelver Shi'i surroundings,[3] but it is clear from the *Sayr wa sulūk* that his parents were not of Ismaili persuasion and that his affiliation with the Ismailis was a later development in his life.

From an early age, Ṭūsī was an avid listener to his family's opinions on the principles and rulings of the *sharī'at*, assuming that apart from strict observance of the religious law there could not be any other path in religion. But his father was not altogether satisfied with a purely prescriptive approach to the faith. He was an open-minded person who had received his own education from his maternal uncle, a student of Tāj al-Dīn Shahristāna (d. 548/1153).[4] Ṭūsī's father wanted him to receive a sound education and encouraged him to study all branches of knowledge and to examine the views of various schools and sects.

One of Ṭūsī's early teachers, chosen by his father, was Kamāl al-Dīn Muḥammad Ḥāsib who, according to Ṭūsī, had been a student of the poet and philosopher Afḍal al-Dīn Kāshānī (d. c. 610/1213–14),[5] and it was under him that he began to study mathematics. But it seems that Kamāl al-Dīn's teaching was not confined to this subject, as he would often find cause to comment on religious matters which aroused Ṭūsī's curiosity. The pupil plied his teacher with numerous questions to which, however, the latter was either unable or unwilling to give specific answers. For instance, Kamāl al-Dīn would sometimes disparage 'those who blindly follow the rules of the *sharī'at*,' but when Ṭūsī wanted to discuss the matter further he would say: 'That which is the core and essence of the truth cannot yet be mentioned to you, for you are young and do not have experience of the world. If you grow up and are successful, seek for it until you attain it.' [§7] It was probably the combined influence of Ṭūsī's father and Kamāl al-Dīn that inspired in him from a very early age an enduring thirst for knowledge. The strength of this vocation became evident shortly after his father's death, when the young man left home 'in search of the truth, intending to acquire the knowledge which guides people to the happiness of the next world.' [§8]

In the *Sayr wa sulūk*, Ṭūsī gives a brief account of his theological and philosophical education, but he does not go into details about the scholars with whom he became acquainted, nor of his studies in mathematics and astronomy which later became important areas of investigation for him. But we know from other sources that Ṭūsī was a precocious learner who travelled far and wide in search of knowledge. By the time he was seventeen or eighteen, he had studied Ibn Sīnā's major philosophical work, *al-Ishārāt wa al-tanbīhāt*, with Farīd al-Dīn Dāmād, attended the lectures of Quṭb al-Dīn Sarakhsī in Nishapur where he is said to have met the famous poet and mystic Farīd al-Dīn 'Aṭṭār (d. 617/1220), and in 614–18/1217–21 he is known to have studied jurisprudence with Mu'īn al-Dīn Sālim b. Badrān Māzinī.[6]

Ṭūsī informs us that although he benefited greatly from his theological studies, he was becoming increasingly disenchanted with his fruitless search for 'the recognition of the True One, the exalted, the most high, and knowledge of the origin and the return.' He appreciated what he had learnt from theologians about the different positions of the sects, but he could not accept their approach to the faith which constituted 'a doctrine in which they blindly imitated their ancestors' and one that was 'entirely confined to practices of the exoteric side of the *sharī'at*.' [§9]

As for the discipline of philosophy, Ṭūsī found it more congenial to his temperament because of the primacy it accorded to reason; but he could not admit the philosopher's claim that, by using the intellect, it was somehow possible to arrive at 'something which is not within its scope,' that is, the knowledge of God. As Ṭūsī continued to ponder this matter further, it gradually dawned on him that since mankind is divided in its great diversity of opinions, the attainment of the truth is not possible through intellect and reason alone but requires the additional intervention of a *mukammil*, an agent of perfection, an authoritative instructor or preceptor who is aware of such knowledge in its very essence. [§12] Thereafter he began to inquire into the main propagators of this doctrine, the Ismailis, although he dared not talk about it to others out of fear of arousing their hostility and prejudice. [§13]

It was around this time that Ṭūsī came to hear about the learning and wisdom of the Ismaili governor of Quhistān, Muḥtashim Shihāb al-Dīn (d. after 644/1246),[7] and sent him a letter requesting the latter's views on some philosophical questions.[8] Although Shihāb al-Dīn declined to enter into a correspondence with him, Ṭūsī had an opportunity to meet the Muḥtashim briefly when he was in the vicinity of Gird Kūh during the course of one of his journeys. [§15]

The turning-point in Ṭūsī's search for knowledge came a few days later in Khurāsān when he accidentally came across a compilation of the *Fuṣūl-i muqaddas* (Sacred Chapters), the sermons and sayings of the Nizārī Ismaili Imam Ḥasan 'Alā Dhikrihi al-Salām (d. 561/1166),[9] which had a profound impact on him: 'I gained endless benefit from those sacred words which are the light of hearts and the illuminator of inner thoughts.' [§15] It was as a result of these encounters and circumstances that Ṭūsī decided to embrace the Ismaili faith. But it was only after persistent efforts on his part and the personal intervention of Nāṣir al-Dīn Muḥtashim (d. 655/1257),[10] who succeeded Shihāb al-Dīn as governor of Quhistān sometime after 621/1224, that Ṭūsī was admitted as a *mustajīb* (novice) into the Ismaili community. [§16] At about this time or shortly thereafter, Ṭūsī joined the service of Nāṣir al-Dīn, thus beginning his close association with the Ismaili leadership which was to continue for more than thirty years of his life.

There has been much speculation among scholars as to the precise nature of Ṭūsī's relationship with the Ismailis and whether it was motivated by religious allegiance or purely professional considerations. The information that Ṭūsī gives in the *Sayr wa sulūk* leaves little doubt of his genuine conversion to the Ismaili faith. It is significant to note here that some of the people responsible for Ṭūsī's education besides his father and maternal uncle, such as Tāj al-Dīn Shahrastānī, Afḍal al-Dīn Kāshānī and Kamāl al-Dīn Muḥammad Ḥāsib, were associated with the Ismailis in one way or another, or they were inclined towards the spiritual and esoteric understanding of Islam as advocated by the Ismailis.

In Quhistān, Ṭūsī appears to have developed a close personal and professional relationship with his Ismaili patron, Nāṣir al-Dīn Muḥtashim. A highly learned man with a special interest in ethical philosophy, Nāṣir al-Dīn had prepared an outline of a book on ethics but was unable to complete it because of the burdens of his administrative duties as the governor of Quhistān. He therefore turned to his young protégé who had earlier expressed an interest in completing the work, and in whose scholarship he had clearly a great deal of trust and confidence. The book was not meant to be an independent work by Ṭūsī, but based on the Muḥtashim's notes and instructions. Hence, when the work was completed, Ṭūsī named it *Akhlāq-i Muḥtashimī* (The Muhtashimid Ethics).[11]

During the next ten years or so that Ṭūsī stayed in Quhistān, he composed a number of other works, such as *Gushāyish-nāma* (Unveiling Notes)[12] on ethics and *Risāla-yi Mu'īniyya* (The Mu'inid Treatise)[13] on astronomy. In 633/1235, he completed the first version of his most famous work on ethics, *Akhlāq-i Nāṣirī* (The Nasirean Ethics).[14] Many other treatises, including *Tawallā wa tabarrā* (Solidarity and Dissociation) and *Āghāz wa anjām* (The Beginning and the End)[15] should probably be dated to this period of his life.

It was shortly after the completion of 'The Nasirean Ethics' that Ṭūsī accompanied Nāṣir al-Dīn Muḥtashim to the central Ismaili strongholds of Alamūt and Maymūn Dizh, situated in the Rūdbār district of Daylamān province in northern Iran. There are several spurious stories about Ṭūsī's move, including one that he was coerced to go on account of the discovery of his secret correspondence with the 'Abbāsid authorities in Baghdād.[16] But the most likely explanation is that the journey to Alamūt was one of the regular visits made by Nāṣir al-Dīn to the Ismaili headquarters in order to report in person on administrative affairs, and it was natural for the governor to take along with him a number of his most trusted confidants. In any case, Ṭūsī would have regarded the journey as a matter of great honour and opportunity, especially as Alamūt was the seat of the Ismaili Imams, it housed the most important library in the Ismaili state, and it offered refuge to many scholars, Sunni and Shi'i alike, fleeing from the Mongol invasions of Central Asia and Khurāsān.

Whatever plans and aspirations Ṭūsī may have had, his lengthy stay of some twenty years in Alamūt and Maymūn Dizh was probably the most productive period of his life. His creativity seems to have flourished under the patronage of the Imam 'Alā' al-Dīn Muḥammad (d. 653/1255)[17] and the elite of the

Ismaili community of the time. It appears that Ṭūsī enjoyed a great deal of intellectual freedom, enabling him to write on a variety of subjects, including astronomy, mathematics, philosophy and various branches of the applied sciences. Ṭūsī completed the most important of his philosophical works on Ismaili thought, *Rawḍa-yi taslīm* (Paradise of Submission),[18] in 640/1242 and *Asās al-iqtibās* (Principles of Acquisition) in 642/1244.[19] His famous defence of Ibn Sīnā against the criticism of Fakhr al-Dīn al-Rāzī, *Sharḥ al-ishārāt wa al-tanbīhāt* (Commentary on the Book of Directives and Remarks),[20] received its final touches in 644/1246. These are in addition to numerous works on astronomy and translations which were produced in his final years at Alamūt.[21] It is probably as a result of these literary efforts, among other factors, that Ṭūsī was honoured with the title of *sulṭān al-du'āt*.

Ṭūsī's early years at Alamūt must have been fairly secure and tranquil in so far as his personal and scholarly life was concerned, but his later writings reflect increasing signs of anxiety arising from the approaching threat of the Mongols. Having overwhelmed Central Asia and northern Khurāsān, the Mongols were now making preparations to invade Iran with the avowed aim of annihilating the Ismaili strongholds as their first priority. Already by 651/1253 several Ismaili fortresses in Quhistān had been overrun and captured. In 654/1256 the Mongol warlord Hūlāgū himself arrived in Rūdbār and laid seige to Alamūt and Maymūn Dizh. After protracted skirmishes and negotiations, the Ismailis finally capitulated and the Mongols commenced a general destruction of their castles, followed by widespread massacres of Ismaili populations in the country at large. As for Alamūt, the centre of the Ismaili state founded by Ḥasan Ṣabbāḥ 166 years earlier, it was systematically torched and dismantled, although the historian 'Aṭā Malik Juwaynī (d. 681/1282), who had accompanied the conquerors, was allowed to salvage a few books and astronomical instruments from its library.[22]

Ṭūsī's role in these fateful events is perhaps the most confusing and controversial aspect of his life. As a senior member of the Ismaili team negotiating with the Mongols, he had advocated peaceful surrender in oppositon to those who had argued for continued resistance from their fortresses in the same way as they had held out for so long against the Saljūqs and the Khwārazmians. Nonetheless, shortly after the fall of Alamūt, Ṭūsī disassociated himself from the Ismailis, claiming that he was held by them against his will, which undoubtedly paved the ground for his preferment in the Mongol court. Ṭūsī has been further accused of encouraging Hūlāgū to invade Baghdād in spite of the latter's superstitious dread of divine retribution if he were to shed the blood of the 'Abbasid caliph.[23]

Ṭūsī's apparent renunciation of the Ismailis and his defection to the Mongols raise a number of questions which are central to any assessment of his life and works. What role did he play in the fall of Alamūt and the destruction of Ismaili power in Iran? Was he all along a Twelver Shi'i who encouraged the Ismailis to surrender and the Mongols to overthrow the pro-Sunni 'Abbāsids in order to ensure the ascendancy of his co-religionists? Was Ṭūsī perhaps still an Ismaili, giving expression to the principle of *taqiyya* (dissimulation) in the hope of a resurgence of Ismaili fortunes? Or is Ṭūsī's case simply one of personal opportunism and professional ambition? These are some of the questions to which it is difficult to find clear and precise answers, as is evident in the diversity of opinions among scholars regarding Ṭūsī's intentions and actions.[24]

The transference of Ṭūsī's loyalty to the Mongols was well-placed for him at least on one count, for he succeeded in persuading his new patrons to finance the construction of a great new observatory at Marāgha in Azarbayjan.[25] Ṭūsī devoted the last decade of his life to supervising this ambitious project, preparing astronomical tables and organizing its library, in addition to his administrative duties in the Mongol court. However, such preoccupations did not prevent him from writing several treatises on philosophical theology, such as *Muṣāri al-muṣāri'* (Downfall of the Wrestler)[26] and *Talkhīṣ al-muḥaṣṣal* (Summary of the *Muḥaṣṣal*),[27] as well as works in in support of Twelver Shi'ism, such as *Risālat al-imāma* (Treatise on

Imamate)[28] and *Tajrīd al-i'tiqād* (Abstraction of Belief).[29]

Yet Ṭūsī was never able to dispense altogether with the Ismaili ideas he had imbibed so deeply and for so long. In fact, the philosophical impetus arising from his acquaintance with Ismaili thought remained a major influence to the last years of his life. In the second edition of *Akhlāq-i Nāṣirī*, although Ṭūsī deleted the introductory eulogy of the Imam 'Alā' al-Dīn Muḥammad and Nāṣir al-Dīn Muḥtashim, he did not revise the work substantially and retained its Ismaili mode of expression.[30] In the *Qawā'id al-'aqā'id* (Canon of Beliefs),[31] he gave a far more elaborate and precise account of Ismaili principles than of Twelver Shi'ism, some of which is a word-for-word translation in Arabic of what he had said earlier in the *Sayr wa sulūk*. Similarly, in his Sufi treatise, the *Awṣāf al-ashrāf* (Attributes of the Illustrious),[32] Ṭūsī retains an Ismaili viewpoint, especially on the subject of spiritual union. In the *Talkhīṣ al-muḥaṣṣal*, which was his last work composed in 669/1271, he even appears to defend the Ismaili doctrine of *ta'līm* while seeming to correct Fakhr al-Dīn al-Rāzī's misrepresentation of it,[33] and rejects the possibility of *badā'* (detraction) of the *naṣṣ* (formal designation) of an Imam as maintained by the Twelver Shi'is. In the light of such tendencies, as well as his long journey around the year 665/1266 to Quhistān, where among the Ismaili population the remnants of his own family may have survived,[34] it is possible that Ṭūsī did not altogether cut off his relations with the Ismailis of Iran after the fall of Alamūt.

Sayr wa sulūk

It is a common phenomenon in all religions for certain individuals whose beliefs and attitudes have undergone a radical transformation to write accounts of their spiritual growth and conversions. There are many examples of such autobiographical writings in religious literature. In the Christian tradition, the classic example is that of St Augustine (d. 430 CE).[35] In all such narratives, there is common ground in the author's attempt to present a rational understanding of the circumstances leading to his or her spiritual transformation, including a justification of the new faith and a refutation of other competing creeds.

Among the best specimens of this genre in Islamic literature are *al-Munqidh min al-ḍalāl* (Redemption from Error) by al-Ghazzālī (d.505/1111) in Arabic and Ṭūsī's *Sayr wa sulūk* in Persian. There are also numerous confessional poems, such as the *Qaṣida-yi i'tirāfiyya* of Nāṣir Khusraw (d. after 465/1072),[36] which give expression to the same kind of religious experience. In the case of both al-Ghazzālī and Ṭūsī, their conversions took place against the background of one of the great debates that engaged the minds of Muslim thinkers for several centuries, namely the relation between reason and revelation, and whether it is possible for human beings to attain the ultimate truths of religion. For al-Ghazzālī, the eminent Sunni jurist and theologian who was preoccupied with this issue for much of his life, the central question was the relative merits of scholastic theology (*kalām*), philosophy (*ḥikmat*), authoritative teaching (*ta'līm*) and mysticism (*taṣawwuf*) for the acquisition of this body of truths.[37] After a long period of deliberation and seclusion, al-Ghazzālī came to favour the Sufi path, although in the *Munqidh* he was unable to refute the principle of *ta'līm* as such, for he recognized in it the rationale for the necessity of prophethood. For Ṭūsī, however, who came a century later and for whom Sufism was not incompatible with Shi'ism, the choice was essentially between speculative philosophy and the guidance of an authoritative teacher, and the process of resolving this conflict forms the subject matter of the *Sayr wa sulūk*.

In his edition of the text, Mudarris Raḍawī says that the manuscript bears no title and was designated as *Sayr wa sulūk* by whoever first published it. However, a glance at the contents of the treatise recounting the author's conversion process demonstrates the appropriateness of the title.[38] In any case, the *Sayr wa sulūk* ranks among the most important of Ṭūsī's works because of the unique information it contains on the author's early life, education and spiritual conversion, as well as for the clear and vivid insights it provides of Ismaili thought towards the closing decades of the Alamūt period in Ismaili history. It is on account of this autobiographical and other internal evidence that Ṭūṣī's authorship of the text has now come to be clearly recognized by a majority of leading scholars.[39]

The *Sayr wa sulūk* takes the form of an extended letter written by Ṭūsī and addressed to the 'chief of the *dāʿīs* and ministers,' [§2] Muẓaffar b. Muḥammad,[40] to be delivered to him through the intermediary of Muẓaffar b. Mu'ayyad. Not much is known about the first Muẓaffar other than what Ṭūsī tells us in his eulogy of the chief *dāʿī*, but the second Muẓaffar referred to as 'the great governor' [§4] in all probability is none other than his patron in Quhistān, Nāṣir al-Dīn Muḥtashim. Since the letter is submitted through Nāṣir al-Dīn, and Ṭūsī admits that he had not yet had the good fortune of meeting the chief *dāʿī*, this indicates that Ṭūsī may have composed the epistle in the Ismaili stronghold of Qā'in in Quhistān and subsequently revised it in Alamūt or Maymūn Dizh sometime after 644/1246, following the death of his old friend Shihāb al-Dīn.[41]

The letter is clearly intended to be autobiographical and confessional, that is, to convey an account of Ṭūsī's personal search for knowledge which led him to embrace the Ismaili faith, together with a declaration of his religious convictions. But the philosophical and theological content of the work gives it special importance in the collection of Ṭūsī's writings that have come down to us because the author has clearly an expository purpose which manifests itself in his highly skilful elaboration of the doctrine of *taʿlīm*.

The principle of *taʿlīm*, that is the authoritative religious guidance of a legitimate Imam, is fundamental to Shiʿi Islam. The elucidation of how mankind can recognize the Imam, who by his very existence substantiates and preserves the truth of faith and religion, is an outstanding feature of Ismaili doctrinal writings. The *Rasā'il Ikhwān al-Ṣafā'* (Epistles of the Brethren of Purity)[42] reflect an early Ismaili attempt. The *Kitāb al-iftikhār* (The Book of Pride)[43] by Abū Yaʿqūb al-Sijistānī (d. after 361/971), the *Rāḥat al-ʿaql* (The Quietude of Intellect)[44] by Ḥamīd al-Dīn al-Kirmānī (d. ca. 411/1020–1), *al-Majālis* (The

Lectures)[45] by al-Mu'ayyad fī al-Dīn al-Shīrāzī (d. 470/1078), and the *Zād al-musafirīn* (The Travellers' Provisions)[46] by Nāṣir Khuṣraw – to name but a few Fatimid Ismaili sources – are all in various degrees devoted to this subject. But the person who has come to be most closely associated with the doctrine of *ta'līm* is the *dā'ī* Ḥasan Ṣabbāḥ (d. 518/1124).

Commonly referred to as Bābā Sayyidnā by the Nizārī Ismailis of the Alamūt period, Ḥasan Ṣabbāḥ was the architect of the Ismaili state in Iran.[47] It was Ḥasan who reformulated the doctrine of *ta'līm* into a powerful intellectual tool to prove the necessity of a supreme guide for mankind, which became the central feature of what al-Shahrastānī calls 'the new preaching' (*al-da'wa al-jadīda*). Although the text of Ḥasan Ṣabbāḥ's exposition of this doctrine, *al-Fuṣūl al-arba'a* (The Four Chapters), has not survived, it is possible to conceptualize the gist of it from the summary of Ḥasan's four propositions given in al-Shahrastānī's heresiographical work, *Kitāb al-milal wa al-niḥal.*[48]

From the evidence of al-Shahrastānī's condensed account, it seems that Ḥasan Ṣabbāḥ's original text must have been a highly forceful and sustained piece of work. In fact, the intellectual challenge it posed to the Sunni establishment under the Saljūqs was serious enough to provoke al-Ghazzālī to refute it in several of his treatises.[49] But al-Shahrastānī devotes only a few pages to the doctrine in the *Milal*, which makes it difficult to follow Ḥasan's finely balanced dialectical process of reasoning. It is therefore to the works of Naṣīr al-Dīn Ṭūsī, in particular the *Sayr wa sulūk* and *Rawḍa-yi taslīm,*[50] that we must turn for a more elaborate and coherent treatment of the subject.

Needless to say, Ṭūsī's purpose, approach and treatment of the subject are different from those of Ḥasan. His arguments, though not presented in the syllogistic style of Ḥasan, are rigorous in their demonstration of deductive logic and proofs, drawing upon a wide array of evidence from theological and philosophical sources. Moreover, the ontological and epistemological framework in which he posits the doctrine is something we do not apparently find in Ḥasan's exposition. At the same time, there is much in common between the two accounts, and Ṭūsī's presentation must therefore be seen as a development of Ḥasan's earlier formulations. As such, Ṭūsī's work represents the Ismaili doctrine of *ta'līm* in the fullness of its maturity as it evolved more than a century after Ḥasan Ṣabbāḥ articulated it.

The *Sayr wa sulūk* is composed in a highly condensed and abstract style typical of medieval scholastic texts. This aspect may be deliberate and intentional for the reason that Ṭūsī was writing a personal and confidential letter to the chief Ismaili *dā'ī*, Muẓaffar b. Muḥammad who, like Ṭūsī's patron Nāṣir al-Dīn, was an accomplished man of learning, fully grounded in the intellectual and religious discourse of his time. Since the text was addressed to the top leadership of the Ismaili community, including possibly the Imam of the time, and there is no evidence that it was intended to serve as a textbook for the Ismaili *da'wat*, it raises the question as to the author's real motives in narrating his 'innermost secrets of thought' in such a confidential and intimate manner. At the beginning of the letter, Ṭūsī admits to writing it in order to seek the chief *dā'ī*'s 'admonitory guidance about right and wrong, truthfulness and deviation,' but the subtext of the letter may be understood as an expression of Ṭūsī's need to demonstrate in writing to the Ismaili leadership his superior intellectual and scholarly talents which he could bring to serve the cause. Although for a different reason, this is reminiscent of Nāṣir Khusraw's letter to 'Alī b. Aḥmad, a high government official, when he reached the city of Baṣra in 443/1051.[51] But there is every reason to believe that Ṭūsī's permanent transfer from Quhistān to Alamūt and his subsequent promotion in the Ismaili *da'wat* could not have been possible without a good opinion of him generated by the submission of this letter.

Leaving aside his intentions for writing the *Sayr wa sulūk*, in this autobiographical account Ṭūsī makes a clear distinction between two major phases in his search for the truth, which he terms the exoteric and the esoteric. In the exoteric phase, corresponding broadly with his early theological and philosophical studies, Ṭūsī is mainly concerned with rational inquiry based on the premise that it is possible to attain the knowledge of God by intellect and sound reasoning alone. The critical turning-point of this phase appears to have been his recognition of the limits of speculative reason and its contradictory results, vis-à-vis his growing awareness that the supra-rational nature of the knowledge he was seeking cannot be attained without the intervention of an authoritative teacher. The esoteric phase of Ṭūsī's quest develops after his meeting with Shihāb al-Dīn and his acquaintance with the *Fuṣūl-i muqaddas,* the sermons of the Imam Ḥasan 'Alā Dhikrihi al-Salām, which led to his conversion to the Ismaili faith.

Ṭūsī depicts this process in terms of a series of progressive stages and the uncovering of a number of veils leading to what he calls '*ilm-i yaqīnī* (reliable or certain knowledge). He characterizes this phase as esoteric, partly because it was based upon or derived from the teachings of the Ismaili *da'wat* which became accessible to him only after his conversion, but more importantly because for Ṭūsī it represents a succession of contemplations upon the inner meanings of the principle of a universal teacher accessible to humankind.

In the course of disclosing these 'unveilings', Ṭūsī embarks on a systematic elaboration of the doctrine of *ta'līm.* He speaks of the necessity of an authoritative teacher [§ 8–13], the qualities of such a teacher and how he may be recognized [§ 17–37], the nature of his teachings and how one may attain perfection through his knowledge [§ 39–49], and the characteristics of the true religion and of its followers among mankind [§ 50–57]. The scope of this introduction does not permit a replication of Ṭūsī's highly complex and nuanced sequence of arguments, inferences and proofs. It is left to the reader to explore the full dimensions of Ṭūsī's thought in his own inimitable style in the Persian language or its translation which, as the readers may find, is a close rendering of the original text.

There are, however, several aspects of Ṭūsī's thought as recounted in the *Sayr wa sulūk, Rawḍa-yi taslīm* and his other Ismaili works which deserve close scrutiny by scholars of Ismaili thought and literature. For example, there is need to establish the relationship of Ṭūsī's thinking with Ḥasan Ṣabbāḥ's formulation of the doctrine of *ta'līm,* in both its historical and ideological settings. It is also essential to situate this doctrine within the broader context of the preaching of the *qiyāmat* (resurrection), which characterized Ismaili thought of the later Alamūt period and to which Ṭūsī makes a number of elusive references in his works. A comprehensive study of the principle of *ta'līm,* its place in the Ismaili literature of pre-Fatimid and Fatimid eras, and its subsequent development in the intellectual tradition of Alamūt, would enable us to ascertain the contributions of Ḥasan Ṣabbāḥ and Ṭūsī to the evolution of the doctrine, and of the extent to which it was a reformulation and elaboration of an old Shi'i precept.

At a more specific level, scholarly investigations can focus upon particular facets of Ṭūsī's ontological system, for instance his understanding of the *amr* (command) or *kalima* (word) of God. This concept featured prominently in Fatimid Ismaili metaphysical thought, at least since the time of Muḥammad al-Nasafī and Abū Ya'qūb al-Sijistānī in the fourth/tenth century, although Ḥamīd al-Dīn al-Kirmānī later disputed their notion of the divine command as intermediary between God and the first intellect.[52] Ṭūsī's re-emphasis on the *amr* and its symbolic correspondence with the universal teacher, in terms of the *maẓhar* (locus, representation or manifestation) of the command, is a significant aspect of his writings that has come to be associated with Ismaili literature of the Alamūt period in general.

Another dimension of the *Sayr wa sulūk* which deserves critical study is Ṭūsī's sophisticated and multi-layered theory of divine knowledge in its application to both the seeker and the source of the knowledge. This may turn out to be the most original contribution of Ṭūsī to the doctrine of *ta'līm.*

The *Sayr wa sulūk* has two interconnected facets: one is autobiographical and confessional, concerned with Ṭūsī's personal search for knowledge from the time of his youth to his conversion to the Ismaili faith; the other is doctrinal, in which the author sets out to demonstrate rationally, on the basis of a series of proofs and arguments, that true or certain knowledge of the divine is attainable only through the mediation of a universal teacher, who cannot be non-existent and must be recognizable among mankind. In the presentation of both these facets, Ṭūsī's work emerges as one of the most important documents of Persian Ismaili literature. In the author's personal candour, lucidity of thought, sensitive treatment of the subject and epistolary style, it stands out among the finest works of intellectual biography in Islamic literature. At a theological and philosophical level, the *Sayr wa sulūk* provides unique insights into the character of Ismaili thought towards the end of the Alamūt period. Ṭūsī's exposition of the ontological, epistemological and spiritual dimensions of *ta'līm*, and the harnessing of these perspectives into a coherent system of thought, makes it by far the most sophisticated treatment of the subject available to us today.

Ṭūsī's other Ismaili works

The three decades during which Ṭūsī was associated with the Ismailis, from around 620/1224 to 654/1256, were undoubtedly the most productive period of his life.[53] The greater part of his works on philosophy and science were produced under Ismaili patronage. Since the bulk of what Ismaili scholars produced in the Alamūt period perished following the collapse of Ismaili political power, the few specimens which have survived cannot tell us the whole story or enable us to assess the conditions in which Ṭūsī produced these works. What is remarkable, and perhaps unique, in Muslim history is the attitude of the Ismaili leaders who, while being involved in an epochal life and death struggle, nevertheless had time to nurture and maintain a very high standard of scholarship within the confines of their castles and fortresses. We know that the leadership consisted of people with a genuine love for learning and scholarship. The fame of the Alamūt library and its treasure of scientific instruments had reached far and wide, and the threat of Mongol invasions was in itself a factor to encourage scholars, both Muslim and non-Muslim, to take refuge with the Ismailis. But at the same time, life in the fortresses was not without its personal and scholarly privations. Thus, when Ṭūsī was drafting the most important chapter of *Rawḍa-yi taslīm*, he notes: 'One should not write everything, especially in times like these, hastily, secretly, and in a dark place ...'[54]

Whatever the circumstances, it is fortunate that a good portion of what Ṭūsī produced during his Ismaili period has survived, whereas nothing has been preserved from, for example, the numerous writings of the Imam Nūr al-Dīn Muḥammad (d. 607/1210) which were very popular at the time.[55] Among other factors, the survival of Ṭūsī's works was undoubtedly due to the scholarly appeal of his writings, which brought him fame in his own lifetime. Since most of his works in Arabic and Persian were not addressed to a specifically Ismaili audience, we can assume that they circulated freely among the scholars and savants of all communities before, as they did after, the fall of Alamūt. It is on the basis of these works, concerned essentially with issues and questions of interest to Muslim intellectuals in general and all those genuinely seeking knowledge, that Ṭūsī's considerable reputation as a scholar is founded. Nonetheless, many of these works retain a certain Ismaili outlook and orientation which, in conformity with the author's ecumenical spirit, is conveyed implicitly within an intellectual context acceptable to the various communities of Islam.

From the point of view of Ismaili studies, Ṭūsī's most important contribution was the scholarly preservation and rendering of the Ismaili tenets and principles of the Alamūt period, which have survived to our time almost exclusively in a number of treatises he wrote for the Ismaili *da'wat* in the Persian language. In addition to the *Sayr wa sulūk* and his ethical works composed under Ismaili sponsorship, the *Akhlāq-i Nāṣirī* and the *Akhlāq-i Muḥtashimī*, there are at least four major treatises by Ṭūsī which should be considered as Ismaili in character.

Āghāz wa anjām

Composed in Quhistān, the *Āghāz wa anjām* (The Beginning and the End),[56] or *Tadhkira* (Exhortations) as Ṭūsī calls it, is his most important work on eschatology. It is divided into twenty chapters dealing with life in the physical and spiritual worlds, the origin and return of the human soul, the phenomenon of death, the nature of the hereafter and the condition of different classes of people therein, the resurrection and the judgement, reward and punishment, heaven and hell, and a number of other Qur'ānic concepts about the afterlife. Ṭūsī's main concern is to elucidate the esoteric meanings and ethical underpinnings of Qur'ānic eschatology from a typically Ismaili point of view. Based on what Ṭūsī writes in *Rawḍa-yi taslīm* and *Āghāz wa anjām*, a comprehensive picture of Ismaili eschatology can be drawn. Among the Twelver Shi'i scholars, the *Āghāz* received special attention from Ṣadr al-Dīn Shīrāzī, better known as Mullā Ṣadrā (d. 1050/1640), who incorporated an Arabic translation of the entire text in his famous commentary on the Qur'ān, *Mafātīḥ al-ghayb*,[57] without acknowledging his source.

Tawallā wa tabarrā

The Qur'ānic concept of *tawallā wa tabarrā* (solidarity and dissociation) which provides the title of this work,[58] occupied an important place in the Ismaili theological framework of the Alamūt period. Ṭūsī refers to it in several of his works and composed this treatise around 633/1253 to elaborate the doctrine in some detail. Dedicated to Nāṣir al-Dīn Muḥtashim, it describes how one may arrive at spiritual perfection through 'solidarity' with 'Alī and the Imams, and 'dissociation' from one's base instincts such as lust, anger and hatred. Through a combination of these two dispositions, one can transmute the passions into yearning, love and *ma'rifat* (gnosis). Ṭūsī stresses the importance of the intellect and rational soul in bringing about this transformation, the outcomes of which are *riḍā* (contentment), *taslīm* (submission) and *īqān* (certitude). For the man of certitude, says Ṭūsī, hatred is submerged into love, the 'primordial past' into the 'subsequent future', and religious law into the realm of resurrection.[59]

Maṭlūb al-mu'minīn

Ṭūṣī wrote the *Maṭlūb al-mu'minīn* (Provisions for the Faithful)[60] in Alamūt or Maymūn Dizh in response to the request of the 'august presence' (*haḍrat-i 'ulyā*) of a noble lady from the house of the Imam 'Alā' al-Dīn Muḥammad who wanted the author to compile the gist of what he had read from the *Fuṣūl-i muqaddas* of the Imam Ḥasan 'Alā Dhikrihi al-Salām and other *da'wat* literature. The book has four chapters dealing with eschatology, the characteristics of an Ismaili (recognition of and love for the Imam, etc.), the doctrine of solidarity and dissociation, and the esoteric exegesis of religious law. In his discussion of the *sharī'at*, Ṭūsī insists that the *mard-i ḥaqīqat* (man of truth) is one who fulfils the requirements of both the *ẓāhir* and the *bāṭin* of the religious law.

Rawḍa-yi taslīm

The *Rawḍa-yi taslīm* (The Paradise of Submission)[61] is Ṭūsī's most important and extensive Ismaili work. It consists of twenty-eight 'representations' or chapters (*taṣawwurāt*) on a variety of themes such as the Creator *(āfarīdagār)* and the cosmos, the nature of human existence, ethics and human relations, religion, eschatology, Prophethood and Imamate. The arrangement of material in the work leads the reader progressively from an understanding of the physical to the spiritual worlds. The twenty-seventh representation deals with pre-Islamic religions such as Sabaenism and idol-worship in the Indian subcontinent. The final *taṣawwur* stands out on its own as it contains responses, some of them recorded only partially, of the Imam 'Alā' al-Dīn Muḥammad to certain inquries put to him by Ṭūsī or others. The significance of this work arises from its comprehensive treatment of Ismaili thought during the Alamūt period, as well as a number of direct references to the teachings of the Imam Ḥasan 'Alā Dhikrihi al-Salām and the preaching of the resurrection. The *Rawḍa-yi taslīm* also contains Ṭūsī's articulation of a distinctively Ismaili system of ethics centred around the recognition of the Imam of the time.

Minor works

It is now certain that during his long association with the Ismailis, Ṭūsī wrote a number of other Ismaili treatises. These works either have not survived or their Ismaili orientation may have been altered by later scholars or scribes to adapt them to Twelver Shi'i milieux. An example of such an amended text is *Riṣāla-yi jabr wa qadar* (Treatise on Free Will and Predestination),[62] a philosophical work in which quotations from the *Fuṣūl-i muqaddas* of the Imam Ḥasan 'Alā Dhikrihi al-Salām have been removed. *Al-Dustūr wa da'wat al-mu'minīn li al-huḍūr* (Notebook for Summoning the Faithful to the Present Imam)[63] is another treatise which, although attributed by the compiler to the Imam 'Alā' al-Dīn Muḥammad, is almost certainly the work of Ṭūsī himself. It gives a detailed account of the ceremonies conducted for conversion to the Ismaili faith, which is described as 'the religion of the theosophers and those travelling in the path of the scholars of divinity who are followers of the House of Prophethood.'

There are also several other extant Ismaili works by Ṭūsī which, apart from the *Mujārāt-i Ṭūsī* (Ṭūsī's Debates),[64] I have been unable to obtain. These are *Jawāb bi Kīyā Shāh Amīr* (Answers to Kīyā Shāh Amīr) and *Riṣāla dar ni'mat-hā, khushī-hā wa ladhdhat-hā* (Treatise on Comfort, Happiness and Joyfulness).[65]

Naṣīr al-Dīn Ṭūsī

CONTEMPLATION AND ACTION

O Lord,
Thou hast bestowed Thy grace,
mayest Thou increase it.
Our Lord, give us mercy from Thee,
and furnish us with rectitude in our affair (18:10).

[§1] The greatest blessing and the most abundant generosity which [is bestowed] in these times [on] all the servants of the lord of the age (*khudāwand-i zamān*),[1] the legitimate [Imam] of this epoch, the rightful leader, the manifestation of the word of God in the two worlds, the master of the 'two weighty things' (*thaqalayn*),[2] the guardian of the east and the west – may God exalt his word (*kalima*) and spread his summons (*da'wat*) over all the earth – belongs to the exalted personage to whose reliable authority and capable hands has been entrusted the control of administrative affairs; [he who is] the pole of truth and religion, the paragon of knowledge in this world, the most perfect exemplar of the human race, Muẓaffar b. Muḥammad[3] – may God extend the shadow of his splendour and protect the lights of his perfection – whose world-adorning opinion maintains the wise order of the two worlds, and whose unravelling mind interprets the divine secrets. 'When God the exalted desires good for a people, He entrusts the rule to its men of knowledge, and knowledge to its rulers.'[4] May God, the glorious, the exalted, preserve this wholesome favour forever, facilitate its acknowledgement, and bestow success on everyone so that they may be grateful [for it]. He is the most kind, the most responsive.[5]

[§2] For some time, this most humble servant,[6] Muḥammad al-Ṭūsī, has been wishing to submit a description of his religious beliefs and a short account of the story of his life to the truth-revealing opinion of the exalted presence of [Muẓaffar b. Muḥammad] the chief of *dāʿīs* and ministers (*sulṭān al-duʿāt wa al-wuzarāʾ*) – may he remain lofty – so that this supreme presence, who is the source of instruction for the secrets of wisdom (*ḥikmat*) and the manifestation of the lights of compassion, may bestow the honour of admonitory guidance about right and wrong, truthfulness and deviation, in accordance with the aptitude of this humble servant, indicating that which is required for his welfare in religious and worldly matters.

[§3] My intention was to present the situation in person, after attaining the good fortune of an audience before that blessed presence, so that if, as a result, that glorious court (*bārgāh*) were pleased to give instruction, it would be devoid of the defects of physical intermediaries and be more effective and appropriate. However, the delay [between intention and performance] which the nature of everyday life renders unavoidable, necessitated a postponement. Another reason was that for intelligent people there is no secret which has to be kept more hidden than the secret of belief and religious doctrine.[7] Indeed, what harmful consequences would follow if the ordinary, ignorant folk were to become aware of these things requires no explanation. Therefore, I was reluctant to note [my ideas] down and reveal them in writing, thereby endangering my life. But when this postponement extended far beyond what was acceptable, I began deliberating about the onslaught of the 'appointed time' (*ajal*) – 'When their appointed time is reached, they can neither delay nor advance a single moment' (7:34) – and became afraid that, God forbid, precaution in these matters could be the cause of grave calamities, and that if [a person's life] were suddenly to come to an end with one of the most important religious [duties] left undone, then his death would be the death of the ignorant.[8]

[§4] Thus, with sincere intention and a firm determination, I noted down my innermost secrets of thoughts and submitted them, through [the mediation of] my respected friend,[9] before the exalted presence of the great governor, the assister of the state and the world, the king of [all] the chiefs in both the worlds, the pride of the human race, Muẓaffar ibn Mu'ayyad[10] – may his elevated rank endure forever – whose kindness and diligence in protecting the secrets of the sincere (*mukhliṣān*) was known [to me]; so that when the opportunity presented itself he could bring it to the notice of that noble presence with the addition of whatever he might deem to be advantageous in the two worlds to me, in order that I should not have to hear the rebuke (*khiṭāb*), 'Return you back behind and seek for a light' (57:13), and should not be deprived of the answer of the brilliance and glittering effulgence of that sun of perfection. He [Allāh] is the one who gives reply!

[§5] Before entering into the subject in question, there is a preliminary matter which ought to be mentioned, however audacious it may seem. It is the following: in the exoteric aspect it is the usual practice of those who feel some physical illness or pain to desire a physician who is an expert in the cure of different illnesses and pains, and that they explain to the doctor their apparent condition from the time the disease was first felt right up to the end, so that when he comes to know the causes and the signs he can suggest the correct remedy and avoid what is contra-indicated. Likewise, in the [esoteric] truth, it is a condition for those who want a spiritual doctor to save the secrets of their innermost thoughts from corrupt beliefs and the distress of incorrect ideas, which lead to total destruction and eternal perdition [of the soul], that they should do the same thing. In the presence [of such a person], one should describe the story of his inner life from the earliest stage of thought and discrimination to the point where a [set of] beliefs is formed, so that he [the spiritual doctor] can make him aware of where his opinions are sound and where he has slipped. So this most humble servant has followed this tradition and given some glimpses of the course of his life from the time when he first felt discrimination appearing within himself up to the present day. Although the prolixity that I was trying to avoid proved inevitable, my expectation is that the source of bounty and mine of liberality may bestow pardon and not chastize me for my unwillingly committed faults – God willing; He is the holder of generosity and the bestower of being. Now we shall begin to penetrate the subject at hand.

[§6] As a result of predetermined decree and design (*bi ḥukm-i taqdīr wa ittifāq*), I was born and educated among a group of people who were believers in, and followers of, the exoteric aspects of the religious law (*sharī'at*). The only profession and vocation of my near relatives and kindred was to promulgate the exoteric sciences. From the time that [the faculty] of discrimination began to stir within me, I grew and thrived listening to their opinions about both fundamental principles and derived rulings (*uṣūl wa furū'*) [of Islam]. I assumed that, apart from this way, there could be no other religious teaching or method. But my father, a man of the world who had heard the opinions of different kinds of people and had [received] his education from his maternal uncle, who was one of the attendants and students of the chief *dā'ī* (*dā'ī al-du'āt*), Tāj al-Dīn Shahrastāna,[11] was less enthusiastic about following these regulations. He used to encourage me to study [all] the branches of knowledge, and to listen to the opinions of the followers of [various] sects and doctrines.

[§7] Then it happened that one of the students of Afḍal al-Dīn Kāshī – may God have mercy on him – came to the region. His name was Kamāl al-Dīn Muḥammad Ḥāsib,[12] who had acquired a first-rate knowledge in a variety of philosophical subjects, especially in the art of mathematics; he had previously been a friend and acquaintance of my father. My father suggested that I should learn from him and frequent his company; so I began to study mathematics with him.

Frequently, in the course of speaking – may God have mercy on him – he would deprecate the exotericists, and explain the unavoidable inconsistency of those who blindly follow the rules of the *sharī'at*, and I would find his discourse appealing, but whenever I wanted to get to the bottom of what he was saying, he would refuse, remarking: 'That which is the core and essence of the truth cannot yet be mentioned to you, for you are young and do not have experience of the world. If you grow up and are successful, seek for it until you attain it.' Occasionally, as a piece of advice, he would say: 'It is possible that the truth [may be found] among people who are, in the eyes of the group that you know, the most contemptible people,' and he would quote this verse [in which the unbelievers say to Noah]: 'We see not any following thee but the vilest of us, in their apparent opinion' (11:27). Then he would say: 'You should not pay any attention to whether or not someone has an ugly appearance. If, for example, you find truth with the idolaters, you should listen to them and accept it from them.'

[§8] In short, it became clear to me from being in his company that whatever I had heard or seen up to that time [on religious matters] was without foundation. I understood that the truth was in the possession of another group and that I would have to strive hard to attain it.

Not long after this, worldly affairs required him [Kamāl al-Dīn] to move away from the region. [Also at this time] my father departed from this world, and I left my home in search of the truth, intending to acquire the knowledge which guides people to the happiness of the next world. Following the instructions of my father, I studied every subject for which I could find a teacher. But since I was moved by the inclination of my thoughts and the yearning of my soul to discriminate between what was false and what was true in the differing schools of thought and contradictory doctrines, I concentrated my attention on learning the speculative sciences such as theology (*kalām*) and philosophy (*ḥikmat*).

[§9] When I first embarked upon [the study of] theology, I found a science which was entirely confined to practices of the exoteric side of the *sharī'at*. Its practitioners seemed to force the intellect to promote a doctrine in which they blindly imitated their ancestors, cunningly deducing proofs and evidence for its validity, and devising excuses for the absurdities and contradictions which their doctrine necessarily entailed.

In short, I derived some benefit from enquiring into this science, to the extent that I came to know something of the divergence between the sects. I came to understand that [with regard to] the knowledge of truth and the attainment of perfection on which happiness in the hereafter depends, men of intellect agreed in one way or another, summarily but not in detail, on the affirmation of such a truth and a hereafter. However, there was a primary disagreement about whether one could reach the desired objective solely through intellect and reason, or whether, in addition to these, a truthful instructor (*mu'allim-i ṣādiq*) was required. All people are accordingly divided in this respect into two branches: those who believe in reason (*naẓar*), and those who [in addition to reason] believe in instruction (*ta'līm*). Moreover, those who believe in reason [alone] are divided into different schools – which is in itself a lengthy subject – whereas those who believe in [the necessity of] instruction are a group known as the Ismailis. This was my first acquaintance with the religion of the *jamā'at.*[13]

[§10] As the science of theology proved fruitless, except for an acquaintance [it allowed] with the positions of the adherents to [various] doctrines, I became averse to it, and my enthusiasm to learn [more about] it lost its momentum. Then I started [to study] philosophy. I found this science to be noble and of great benefit. I saw that among the groups [into which] mankind [is divided], the practitioners of this discipline were distinguished by their allocation of a place for the intellect in the recognition of realities, and by their not requiring blind imitation (*taqlīd*) of a particular stand. Rather, in most cases they build the structure of religion in accordance with the intellect, 'except what God wills' (7:188). However, when the discussion reached the desired objective – that is, the recognition of the True One (*ḥaqq*), the exalted, the most high, and knowledge of the origin and the return (*mabda' wa ma'ād*) – I found that they were on shaky foundations in these matters, for the intellect (*'aql*) is incapable of encompassing the giver of intellect (*wāhib-i 'aql*) and the origins (*mabādī*). And because they rely on their own intellect and opinion, they blunder, they speak according to their own conjectures and whims in this field, using the intellect [to arrive] at knowledge of something which is not within its scope.

[§11] To sum up, my heart was not satisfied with what they said in these matters, while my desire to attain the truth was not diminished. In my exposition, I shall mention some more aspects of this matter. Many benefits, however, were obtained from this investigation into philosophy, one of them being that I came to know that if in any existing thing perfection is potential (*bi al-quwwa*), it cannot change from potentiality into actuality by itself without being affected by something outside itself, because if its essence were sufficient to bring that perfection from potentiality into actuality, the change would not be delayed. Indeed, the attaining of that perfection would have been simultaneous with the existence of the essence. We can take bodies as an example of this: motion is [always] potential in them. Without the effect of something else, that motion is never actualized; otherwise all bodies would be in [perpetual] motion. But when another thing exerts an effect on a body, that potential motion (*ḥarakat*) becomes actual. In this case the other is called the 'mover' (*muḥarrik*) and the body is called the 'moved' (*mutaḥarrik*).

[§12] Once this proposition had been established and my soul was satisfied of its truth, my attention was drawn to the point that was made in the science of theology, about the primary disagreement among mankind being whether knowledge of the truth is attainable solely through the intellect and reason, without instruction from any teacher, or whether, in addition to intellect and reason, an instructor is needed. Then I applied the [above] proposition to this situation and found that the truth lay with those who believe in instruction (*ta'līmiyān*), for knowledge and understanding in man is in itself [merely] potential, and its perfection can only be actualized in men of sound natures, [in whom] intellect and reason are to be found, when something external has exerted an effect on them. Thus, this perfection too can inevitably only be actualized by means of the effect of some other thing. [Accordingly], when that other bestows a perfection, the perfection [here] being knowledge (*'ilm*), the bestower, in accordance with the previous law, is called the 'instructor' (*mu'allim*) and the one on whom it is bestowed the 'instructed' (*muta'allim*), by analogy with the 'mover' (*muḥarrik*) and the 'moved' (*mutaḥarrik*).[14]

It thus becomes clear that without the instruction (*ta'līm*) of a teacher (*mu'allim*), and the bringing to perfection (*ikmāl*) by an agent of perfection (*mukammil*), the attainment of the truth is not possible; that mankind, with its great number and differences of opinion, is mistaken in its claim that the truth can be reached solely through the intellect and reason; and that the believers in instruction (*ta'līmiyān*) are therefore correct.

[§13] Once this proposition had become clear, I began to investigate the religion (*madhhab*) of this group. But since I did not know anyone who could describe the nature of their doctrine objectively, and could only hear about their beliefs from people hostile to them, and since I knew that I could not rely on a person's prejudices about his enemy, I was unable to get to know [this group] as I should, and out of fear I was unable to disclose my secret.

[§14] In short, I spent [quite] a period of time thinking about this. Then, in the course of my search, I frequently heard from travellers to the [surrounding] countries about the scholarly virtues of the auspicious master, Shihāb al-Dīn[15] – may God be pleased with him – and his deep insight into different fields of knowledge. Then I sought a suitable opportunity and, through the intermediary of a friend who had an association with him, I sent him a letter containing two or three questions about those points in the discourse of the philosophers which I had found to be contradictory and about which I had some observations of my own. Then I was granted the honour of a reply from him – may God be pleased with him – in the handwriting of the master, the chief scribe, Ṣalāḥ al-Dīn Ḥasan[16] – may his glory endure – and in answer to the questions he said: 'For a reason which can only be explained face to face, I am not [in a position] to convey any scholarly communication [in writing].'

[§15] Shortly after this, I took the opportunity, while on a journey from Iraq to Khurāsān, to pass through the glorious territory of [Gird] Kūh[17] – may God, the exalted, protect it – and for two or three days [was able to] be in Shihāb al-Dīn's company and hear something of the *da'wat* doctrines from his own mouth. I copied down his words and derived much [benefit] from them. Since the requisites for staying with him and remaining in that place had not been prepared – for several reasons which I need not go into – I journeyed on from there to Khurāsān. A few days later, I happened to see a copy, in mediocre handwriting and antiquated paper, of the *Fuṣūl-i muqaddas* (Sacred Chapters) of [the Imam] 'Alā Dhikrihi al-Salām,[18] in the possession of an unworthy person who did not know what it was.

Obtaining [the text] with a ruse, I occupied myself day and night with reading it, and to the extent of my humble understanding and ability, I gained endless benefits from those sacred words which are the light of hearts and the illuminator of inner thoughts. It opened a little my eye of exploration (*chishm-i taṣarruf*) and my inner sight (*dīda-yi bāṭin*) was unveiled.

[§16] Thereafter, my only desire was to introduce myself among the *jamā'at* when the opportunity presented itself. At that time, in accordance with my inward motivation, I made such strenuous efforts that finally I succeeded. Through the good offices of the exalted royal presence of Nāṣir al-Ḥaqq wa al-Dīn[19] – may God exalt him – and his compassionate regard for my improvement, I was granted the good fortune of joining the *jamāʿat* and entry among the ranks of the novices (*mustajībān*) of the *daʿwat*, and thus my situation reached the point where it is now.

Nothing can be gained by the illuminated mind in listening to this story except weariness. However, due to the circumstances already mentioned concerning his [Nāṣir al-Dīn's] cordial nature and sympathy for me, its narration seemed to me to be prudent. If God the exalted is willing, it will be covered with the veil of forgiveness and heard with consideration. This [exposition so far] has been a description of the exoteric situation.

[§17] From an esoteric perspective, however, when I had reached a position where I could understand – by the proof that has already been cited – that it was the followers of instruction who were correct, I concluded with no additional troublesome thinking that the true instructor can only be he who is the instructor of the followers of the truth.[20] This person, through whose teaching souls move from potentiality to actuality, must therefore be the instructor of the Taʿlīmiyān [i.e., the Ismailis].

[§18] Then my mind became preoccupied with considering what particular characteristics would distinguish that instructor from other teachers, and what his instruction would be like. With due submissiveness, I beseeched God the exalted – may His greatness be magnified – to clarify and unveil this question, so that my heart might be appeased. Then I referred [myself] to the intellectual principles which I had already verified and the premises which had been made clear in the *Fuṣūl-i muqaddas*. I combined them, asked questions from here and there, and held discussions and debates with [other] novices (*mubtadīyān*), until gradually, through the stages which I will explain, the scheme of beliefs (*ṣūrat-i iʿtiqādī*) as will be mentioned later on became clear in my mind.

[§19] First, it appeared to me that the instructor through whose mediation the potential perfection of the instructed soul is actualized must [himself] be in a state of actual perfection, because he who is not actually perfect cannot perfect others; and if that perfection had been potential in him and become actualized afterwards, he also would have been in need of another instructor. As necessity dictates (*az jihat-i qaṭ'-i iḥtīyāj*),[21] this would either result in an infinite regression (*tasalsul*), or end up with a teacher who has always been in a state of actual perfection. The evidence for the existence of such a person among humankind can be deduced both from philosophy (*ḥikmat*) and revelation (*sharī'at*).

[§20] As for philosophy, it has been stated by philosophers that the possessor of sacred powers (*quwā-yi qudsiyya*) has absolutely no need to acquire knowledge (*iktisāb*). Indeed, merely by focusing his soul, and without having to go through the process of acquisition and active seeking, realities and knowledge become clear [to him] in their totality. As for revelation, it is maintained by the followers of the exoteric (*ahl-i ẓāhir*) that the possessor of bestowed knowledge (*'ilm-i ladunī*) receives it without the mediation of any instruction.[22]

Consequently, the mind does not reject the necessity of the existence among human beings of an instructor who is the first among instructors and is absolutely perfect. The instructor [is necessary] in order that some may gain perfection through him, and others through the latter, so that the effusion of the supreme bliss (*sa'ādat-i nakhust*) might encompass the next level gradually, according to the order and degree which are ordained by the wisdom of the first origin (*ḥikmat-i mabda'-i awwal*).

[§21] When I passed this stage and another veil had been removed from my mind, I realized that the perfection to which the seeker directs himself is knowledge of the True One, the exalted, the most high, who is the origin of [all] beings. Between Him and the first instructor, whose knowledge of the

True One, the exalted, the most high, is always actual, there cannot exist any intermediary, because if an intermediary is posited, he would first have to come to know the intermediary, and then through him the True One. Knowledge of the True One would also, therefore, be a [mere] potentiality in him, [waiting to be actualized] through someone else. If this were so, this other person would have to be the first instructor, not him. But since we have already supposed him to be the first instructor, so the first instructor is the nearest person to God – may He be praised and exalted.

[§22] It only remained for me [to understand] what his knowledge of God – may He be exalted – would be like. While contemplating this, I remembered that in philosophy, in the section on the soul (*kitāb-i nafs*),[23] it has been proved that the most self-evident knowledge, the surest intelligible thing, is the knowledge that non-material beings have of themselves, in which reasoning and acquisition of knowledge play no part. Moreover, it has been demonstrated in logic, in the apodeictics (*kitāb-i burhān*),[24] that the only certain acquired knowledge (*'ilm-i yaqīnī-yi muktasab*) is that in which the effect becomes known through [its] cause. Whatever does not become known through a proof proceeding from cause to effect is not absolutely certain. In the case under consideration, where the discussion is about the philosopher's knowledge of the first cause (*'illat-i ūlā*), he would have to admit that there can be no certainty about that which has no cause.

[§23] Again, when the philosopher discusses the degrees of existents, he posits the first intellect (*'aql-i awwal*), which is the first effect, as the closest being to the first cause. Necessarily, [the first intellect's] knowledge of the first cause is possible only because it is the first effect. But when [the first intellect] cannot be certain [in this knowledge], how could others expect certainty about it? Here, then, the philosopher has completely shut to himself the door on [reaching] the knowledge of God, which is in truth a disturbing and deplorable situation. This is one of the problems I mentioned at the beginning, which resulted in my dissatisfaction with the principles of the philosophers for arriving at the knowledge of the True One.

The aim of setting out these arguments here is not to show the weakness of the philosophers; it is rather to show how my recollection of these points demonstrates that the level [of knowledge] of the first instructor cannot be the level of the first effect [the first intellect]. In fact, his rank must be higher than that of the first effect, in order that his knowledge of the True One, the exalted, the most high, may be the noblest knowledge.

[§24] Here it is necessary to consider whether or not there can be any intermediary at all between the first effect and the first cause. Among most people of discrimination and reason, it is commonly held that there can be no intermediary between the first effect and the first cause. Now the Taʿlīmiyān believe that all beings issue forth from God, the exalted, who is the first origin (*mabdaʾ-i awwal*), through the mediation of something which, in the terminology of the later scholars of this *jamāʿat*, is called His command (*amr*) or His word (*kalima*). [According to them] the first cause of the universal intellect (*ʿaql-i kull*), which is the first effect, is God's command, because God is altogether beyond (*munazzah*) cause or effect.

It is of [crucial] importance to grasp this point, to verify [its] truth and eliminate falsity, because those who do not realize that it is true remain veiled from the knowledge of the True One. Indeed, whoever thinks over this discussion in fairness will realize that he must come to exactly this verdict, as explained by the followers of instruction (*aṣḥāb-i taʿlīm*) about this matter of which he is ignorant. And this is because the philosopher says that 'from the real one (*wāḥid-i ḥaqīqī*) comes forth only one entity.'[25] For example, if two existents were to issue from it at the same time, the aspect from which the first existent issued would be different from the aspect from which the second issued. Thus, if these two different aspects were included in [the absolute unity of] His essence (*māhiyyat*), He would no longer be the real one. And if the two aspects were external to [the real one], then the discussion about their origin would be concerned with how it is possible for two postulated existents to emerge [from it]. Since both these arguments are invalid, it is obvious that two existents cannot possibly come forth from the real one at the same time. It follows therefore that the first effect is one, and this is the first intellect.

[§25] This explains the philosopher's view, but after this he forgets [the principle] which he knew that when only one existent comes forth from the real one, it comes forth in every respect from the one aspect [of its unity], for if the production of two existents necessitates that there be two aspects, the production of one existent requires that there be one aspect. Thus, if they do not admit this [one] aspect, through which the first effect has come forth from the first origin, it must mean that no existent has issued from it, and hence nothing has come into existence [at all]. It is thus demonstrated on the basis of the philosopher's own arguments, which he must admit, that the existence of this [one] aspect is necessarily proven, but because of his negligence of this point, the path to the recognition of God has been barred to him.

[§26] However, the instructor who had not neglected this aspect named it the 'command' (*amr*) or the 'word' (*kalima*), in accordance with the verse of the Qur'ān: 'Verily, His command, when He desires a thing, is to say to it "Be" and it is' (36:82). This verse makes it clear that the issuing forth of existents from God depends on the expression 'Be' (*kun*), and the word 'verily' (*innamā*) in Arabic serves the purpose of pinpointing [the scope of the expression], thereby making clear that the command is an expression for that word. The proof for the existence of this aspect, which only the people of *ta'līm* have established, can also be deduced from philosophy and revelation (*sharī'at*). However, those who cling to only the exoteric aspects of these two methods remain deprived of, and veiled from, the knowledge of it.

There is no doubt that this aspect, the command or the word [of God] is not something additional to His sacred essence, in so far as He is He, the exalted – otherwise another intermediary would be required for the origination of that one [i.e., the first intellect] – but from the point of view where [the command] is the cause of an effect, it is something additional. This additional entity, in reality, is the cause of the first effect, because cause and effect are two concatenating (*iḍāfī*) entities, in so far as there can be no cause without a corresponding effect, and no effect without a corresponding cause. Whatever is relative is within the scope (*ḥayyiz*) of opposition, because opposition can only exist between two things, and duality is plurality.

[§27] Thus, where there is [a concatenation of] cause and effect, there is no escape from plurality, but plurality cannot be allowed for the first origin of existents, since plurality cannot exist without unity. Such being the case, the first origin, the True One – may His name be exalted – cannot, in so far as He is the first origin, be attributed with cause or effect, existence or non-existence, temporality or eternity, necessity or contingency, nor any of the other kinds of opposition, contradiction or concatenation. He is more glorious and exalted than to be the fount of two opposites, the origin of two contraries, the source of unity and plurality, the cause of the absolvement (*tanzīh*) and non-absolvement (*lā tanzīh*) [of attributes]. He is beyond any attribute by which something could be qualified, whether it be non-existent or existent, negative or positive, relative or absolute, verbal or in meaning (*lafẓī yā ma'nawī*). He is beyond [all this], and also beyond the beyond and so forth.

[§28] There is no doubt that no one maintains such pure unity (*tawḥīd-i ṣirf*), such unconditioned absoluteness (*tanzīh-i maḥḍ*) [of God], except the Ta'līmīyān; and none of the adherents of [the other] sects, nor any of their leaders, except the instructor of this group, has been able to go to the extent of unveiling this secret. This is because others talk about possibilities (*na shāyad buwad wa shāyad buwad*), whereas he speaks from the position of 'I recognize You through You, and You are my Guide to Yourself.'[26]

From this [discussion], it becomes clear that, in the terminology of the philosophers, it is an error to speak of the first cause in relation to God, but it is correct to apply it to His command which is the source of all existents. In fact, whatever attribute has been ascribed to the first cause by distinguished philosophers and people of knowledge (*ahl-i ma'rifat*) among the men of intellect, is a reference to His command, one facet of which is directed to the world of pure, eternal unity, the other to the world of multiplicity and contingency; but God as such is free from, and exalted above, both these facets. As has been expressed in the words of [one of] the leader of the truthful people (*pīshwā-yi muḥiqqān*) – may the mention [of their names] be greeted – 'Whatever pertains to God, pertains to us.'[27] However, the man of truth must not succumb here to either exaggeration (*ghuluw*) or underestimation (*taqṣīr*), because the pitfalls are many and the straight path, the true religion of God, which proceeds between underestimation and exaggeration, is narrower than a hair and sharper than a sword-edge.[28]

[§29] In connection with this [matter], a story from my own past experience has come to my mind. Although it may prolong this discourse, I shall relate it, so that, God willing, in accordance with the vindication proffered at the beginning, I may receive the necessary guidance. At that time, when I had not yet joined the *jamā'at*, and had not yet acquired much understanding of the true religion (*madhhab-i ḥaqq*), I was engaged in a dispute with a jurist (*faqīh*) in Jājarm.[29] In the course of the debate, the jurist denigrated the Ismailis. I asked the reason for this, and he said that they considered the Imam to be God, because they refer to their Imam with the words 'our lord' (*mawlānā*) which, in their opinion, could not be used except for God. Sometimes they say 'our lord 'Alī' or 'our lord

Muḥammad,' and sometimes [when addressing God] they say and write, 'O Allah, our Lord (*Allāhumma mawlānā*),' and so on. They seek from 'our lord' what should be sought through prayer from God.

I said that if he were to consider the matter fairly, [he would find that] the foundation of their belief (*qā'ida-yi madhhab*) is that, since God cannot be recognized except through the Imam, the relationship of the Imam to God in respect to his guidance is like that between a name and what it names.[30] Do not ordinary people (*ahl-i 'urf*) use the same word both for the name and the named? They call Zayd 'Zayd' and also call his spoken or written name 'Zayd'. It is because of this that one group[31] have imagined the name to be the same as the named. Thus, if the Ismailis use the name of God [i.e., *mawlānā*] for that person who is the guide to God, they are not deviating from the rules of the philologist or from customary practice. For this reason, they are not guilty of exaggeration, and vilification is not appropriate for them. The jurist could give no reply to this argument, and because this vindication [of the Ismailis] was altogether pertinent, he acted fairly and accepted my explanation.

[§30] In terms of the implication of these principles, it became clear that there is a degree higher than that of effects. This is the degree of the [divine] command, which is the first of [all] causes and the origin of [all] degrees. On the one hand, it is an intermediary between the Creator and what is created, while, on the other, it is the final degree, the [point of] return of [all] beings, and the last of [all] existents.

The knowledge of the first, the command of the True One – praise be to Him – in so far as He is He, in other words from the aspect of absolute unity, is the knowledge of God by God (*ma'rifat-i khudā bi khudā*), within the limits of the knowledge [implied in the verse]: 'God bears witness that there is no God except He' (3:18). This is the noblest degree of certainty, the most perfect mode of knowledge, unlike the knowledge of cause through effect which does not give certainty. For the truth about knowledge is, as they have said: 'We have not known You as You should be known,'[32] [and in the words of the Qur'ān]: 'They do not apportion to God what he deserves' (6:91).

[§31] In the sciences of the truth (*'ulūm-i ḥaqīqī*), it has been perceived that beyond the world of the senses there is another world, that of the intellect, which is related to the former in the same way as the soul is to the body. This is why it is called the spiritual world and the other the physical world. Corresponding to each sensible thing in this world is an intelligible entity in that world, and corresponding to each person here is a spirit there, and corresponding to every manifest thing (*ẓāhir*) here, is a hidden one (*bāṭin*) there. Similarly, corresponding to every intelligible entity there is a sensible one here, and corresponding to each spirit there is a person here, and corresponding to each hidden entity there is a manifest one here. That intelligible entity is the source (*maṣdar*) of this sensible one, and this sensible thing is the manifestation (*maẓhar*) of that intelligible one.

For example, if there were a sensible thing here which did not have an intelligible entity corresponding to it there, its appearance would be a deception, like a mirage or the hallucinations from which the delirious or the melancholic suffer. Just as a derivation (*far'*) cannot exist without a basic principle (*aṣl*) [from which it is derived], one should suppose that an intelligible entity which did not have a sensible entity here corresponding to it would be purely fanciful or imaginary with no reality at all, for no existent can be left floating free (*mu'aṭṭal*). Both the perceptible realm (*shahādat*) and the imperceptible realm (*ghaybat*), the creation and the command, that is to say the two worlds, the physical and the spiritual, have been disclosed in the word of the revelation.

[§32] As for the word of the exalted Creator – which is the sustainer of existents in the world and that by which each of them reaches its perfection, originating from it and returning to it – if it had no connection (*ta'alluq*) to the sensible world, the latter would have never come into existence. Since there is such a connection, which is of the same kind and therefore has to be perceptible to the senses, the command and the word must inevitably be manifest in this world, and the locus of its manifestation (*maẓhar*) must be in the form of an individual human being who appears to be like other humans, [one who] is born, grows old and succeeds to the one before him in a continuous line, so that it [the command] will be preserved in perpetuity [among mankind]: 'And had We made him [the Prophet] an angel, We would have certainly made him a man, and disguised [him] before them in garments like their own'[33] (6:9).

In the world of pure spirituality, it [the command] is the possessor of infinite knowledge and power; all forms of knowledge and perfections pour forth from it upon the intellects and souls: 'We were shadows on the right-hand side of the Throne and praised Him, so the angels praised Him.'[34] This being is the command or the word of God; its rank is higher than that of possible things and effects, both of which are obedient and subservient to His command: 'None is there in the heavens and the earth but he comes to the All-merciful as a servant' (19:93). As for God as such, He is above both the worlds; He is free and absolved from [the oppositions of] unity and multiplicity, similarity and differentiation, reality and relativity (*ḥaqīqat wa iḍāfat*): 'Glory be to thy Lord, the Lord of majesty. [He is] above what they describe' (37:180). Any perfection that exists potentially in souls and individuals in the two realms is brought from potentiality to actuality by [His command], by the light of its instruction and the illumination of its guidance: '[Our lord is He] who gave everything its existence, then guided it' (20:50). Since in the beginning the existents came forth from the Command and by it attain their perfection, it is their origin (*mabda'*) and to it is their return (*ma'ād*); it is the first (*awwal*) and the last (*ākhir*), and in it the circle of existence (*dā'ira-yi wujūd*) is completed: 'He is the first and the last, the manifest and the hidden; He has knowledge of all things' (57:3).

[§33] [The command], therefore, has necessarily three aspects: first, it is a person like any other; second, it is the cause, the instructor, the perfect one, and the others are its effects, the instructed, those who are lacking in perfection; and third, it [the command] is itself, and nothing other than it is worthy of being the cause of existence. The case is such that the three realms, which the people of the *da'wat* have named the realm of similitude (*mushābahat*), the realm of differentiation (*mubāyanat*) and the realm of unity (*waḥdat*), refer to these three aspects.[35]

[§34] The proof that the human species is distinguished from other simple and composite species of the sensible world by the manifestation of [the command] among them is this: according to philosophers, the human being is the noblest in the whole of existence, because he is nobler than the other three kingdoms [i.e., mineral, plant and animal], and the three kingdoms are nobler than the elements [i.e., earth, water, air and fire], and the elements are nobler than their own corporeal bases, that is to say, matter and form. Thus, the noblest source has revealed itself in the noblest manifestation.

[§35] On the evidence of the the revealed law (*sharī'at*) and the exoteric side of revelation (*tanzīl*), the trust (*imānat*) which the heavens, the earth and the mountains were unable to accept, was accepted by mankind: 'We offered the trust to the heavens and the earth and the mountains, but they refused to carry it and were afraid of it; and man carried it. Surely he is unjust, ignorant' (33:72). It was [only] after accepting this trust that humankind deserved the prostration of the intimate angels (*malā'ika-yi muqarrabīn*), who are the noblest in creation: 'And when we said to the angels, "Bow yourselves to Adam," they bowed themselves, except Iblis' (2:34). They testified to the descent of the manifestation of the person of divine knowledge (*shakhṣ-i ma'rifat-i bārī*) among the individuals of the human species when he appeared before them, and not among any other species of existents. And since his appearance in this world is because he is its perfection, as long as the world remains it can never be devoid of him: 'If the earth were devoid of the Imam even for a short time, it would be convulsed with all its inhabitants.'[36]

[§36] It is also necessary that the people should have access to the lights of his guidance; otherwise they would be deprived of attaining perfection, and the usefulness of the manifestation would be rendered futile. Since it is necessary in the world of similitude that human beings should succeed one another through a recognized relationship (*'alāqa*), once this relationship which indicates continuity and succession (*ittiṣāl wa ta'āqub*) is disregarded, the means of knowing him will also be closed to the people. The relationship can only be of two kinds, spiritual and physical. The spiritual relationship is the clear appointment (*naṣṣ*) of one by the other, and the physical relationship is that of the child to father by way of succession. Through these two relationships, the close affinity between these individuals becomes known, and [the meaning of the revealed] evidence (*athar*) 'He made it a word enduring among his posterity' (43:28), and of the decree (*ḥukm*) 'the offspring, one of the other' (3:34), becomes clear. By testifying to these two proofs of birth and clear appointment, all the inhabitants of the world have access to the individual who is the locus of the manifestation of that light.

[§37] However, for the elite (*khawāṣṣ*) there is another sign, which is one of the vestiges of the world of unity (*'ālam-i waḥdat*), and this is his uniqueness in the claim of 'I know God through God and I lead people to God.' This claim and call are vouchsafed to no one but him, so that from all the realms of being there may be testimonies to His eternal unity and the proof (*ḥujjat*) of God among the people may be fulfilled: 'Say, to God belongs the conclusive proof' (6:149). Thus, with these premises and propositions, the rank of the first instructor and the particular characteristics by which he is distinguished, such that he is absolutely perfect whereas others are imperfect and in need of him to perfect them, becomes clear.

[§38] It remains to see what his teaching is, and how people can attain perfection through it. At this point, after much deliberation and thought, and going back to an examination of the sayings of the eminent ones [i.e., the Imams], the following points impressed upon my mind.

Firstly, as the philosophers have explained, absolute certainty cannot be achieved by reasoning from effect to cause; but since the highest state [of knowledge] for the speculative rationalists (*ahl-i naẓar*) is to know cause from effect, no rationalist can come to know God.

Also, since knowledge, according to the rationalists, is a picture (*mithāl*) or form (*ṣūrat*), produced from what is known in the mind (*dhāt*) of the knower, and since any picture or form which is thus produced is different from that which is known, the subject's knowledge must, in reality, be the estimated form (*ṣūrat-i mawhūm*) and not what is actually known. For this reason it has been said: 'Everything which you distinguish by your estimation, even in its most precise meanings, is turned away from Him and returned to you; it is fabricated by you and created like you.'[37]

Since worship depends on knowledge and [human] knowledge is like this, what must worship be like? 'Surely you and that which you worship apart from God are fuel for hell; you shall go down to it' (21:98). Such is the ultimate stage the rationalist reaches in his quest for perfection.

[§39] The followers of *ta'līm,* however, believe in the principle (*qā'ida*) that everyone, whatever his degree may be, knows his own instructor, who in turn knows his own instructor, [and so on] to the first instructor, who knows God through God. As a result, everyone also comes to know God through God.

In the *Fuṣūl-i muqaddas* it is written: 'Everyone must know [God] through knowing me, since a person becomes a knower ('*ārif*) through my knowledge and becomes a monotheist (*muwaḥḥid*) through my monotheism. Then the reality of knowledge (*ma'rifat*), union (*ittiḥād*)[38] and oneness (*waḥdat*) comes completely into existence, and the reality of worship becomes evident.' The evidence for such a judgement in the revealed law and the exoteric aspect of revelation is the text (*naṣṣ*) of the Qur'ān: 'Those are they whom God has guided, so follow their guidance' (6:90). And there is also the fact that in the realm of religious law, knowledge of God is not judged by the mere profession of the formula 'There is no god but God,' unless the confession of 'Muḥammad is His Messenger' is added to it.

[§40] From the point of view of philosophy and rational thought, since both the worlds, the manifest (*ẓāhir*) and the hidden (*bāṭin*), are connected with one another, whatever is real (*bi 'ayn*) there has its trace (*athar*) here, and whatever is real here has its trace there. One can therefore make deductions about the state of that world from the state of this world.

Reflection about this world makes it clear that matter is perpetuated through form, for no matter (*mādda*) can exist without form (*ṣūrat*), and that the multiplicity and differentiation of matter too is caused by the multiplicity and differentiation of form, because matter [whatever form it takes] is, in reality and essence, always the same. Consequently, whenever differentiation between these forms is eliminated, they become one with each other. For example, between the form of water and the form of air there is differentiation and multiplicity. But if water is stripped of its watery form and takes an aerial form [as steam], it becomes one with air and there remains no differentiation between them.

It is the same in that [hidden] world where souls, despite their various ranks, emanate from one origin and share in the same essence (*māhiyyat*), but they are perpetuated [individually] by virtue of the forms they acquire, which is the cause of their coming into this world. So if the form which is represented in the soul of the disciple is identical to that which is represented in his instructor's soul, and if his position is such that he knows through the knowledge of his instructor, and the instructor is in agreement with his return, there will be no differentiation and multiplicity between their souls; and when the veil is removed, he will reach his instructor and be united with his oneness, and then he [the disciple] will have reached [his place of] return.

However, if there is differentiation in the forms of the two souls, such that [in] acquiring the form of his soul the disciple follows his own opinion and desire, or blindly imitates someone else who has followed his own opinion and desire, he remains in the darkness of purgatory (*barzakh*), covered by the veil of multiplicity, which is the shadow of existence, [as mentioned in the verse]: 'No indeed; but upon that day they shall be veiled from their Lord' (83:15).

[§41] In this world, no one who seeks something can reach his goal unless, first of all, he has some capital of the same kind as that which he seeks, and subsequently makes the necessary effort. For example, unless a farmer sows seed and cultivates the land, he cannot reap any harvest; if a merchant has no capital and does no business, he makes no profit; unless a hunter provides himself with bait and goes after the prey, he cannot catch anything; and so on and so forth. Similarly in this world, unless the seeker after perfection attains a favour from the primordial decree (*ḥukm-i mafrūgh*), which is equivalent to the merchant's capital – that is, having a pure soul and a sincere heart, as it is said in [the verse] 'Except for him who comes to God with a pure heart' (26:89) – and [unless he] has acquired something from the subsequent decree (*ḥukm-i musta'nif*), which is equivalent to the merchant's profit – that is, an act of submission (*taslīm*) based on the insight (*baṣīrat*) 'And whosoever submits his will to God, being a doer of good, has grasped the firmest handhold' (31:22) – and unless he yokes both of these together and immerses the subsequent in the primordial, he cannot attain the degree of perfection [indicated in the verse]: 'Theirs is the abode of peace with their Lord, and He is their protector (*walī*)' (6:127).[39]

Here [in the physical world] this capital is a kind of premium;

there [in the spiritual world] the believer's descent was created from the light of the True One: 'The believer has been created from the light of God, and knowledge is a light which God has cast into the heart.'[40] If in the beginning, the believer had not been created from the light of God, he would not get as far as the return (*ma'ād*) implied in [the words] 'When God gives the command, He knows it,'[41] since in the return things go back to whence they started.

[§42] To sum up, from these premises and the testimonies of intellect and religious law (*'aqlī wa shar'ī*), it became evident to me that the final steps on the path of the seekers after truth is to be blessed with success in knowing their instructor and to become knowledgeable through his knowledge, as it is expressed in the *Fuṣūl-i muqaddas*: 'Knowledge of God is [through] knowledge of the Imam.'[42]

[§43] When I reached this stage, I realized that the result of my effort and the end of my search is that submission (*taslīm*) which is required by the religion of the followers of *ta'līm*. 'But no, by thy Lord, they will not believe until they make thee [the Prophet] the judge regarding the disagreement between them; then they shall find in themselves no impediment touching thy verdict, but shall surrender in full submission' (4:65). Up to this point, this spiritual traveller had been in the position of reliance on his own judgement; he had been using his own thought, reflection and reasoning, so that through intellectual deduction he may seek the original instructor (*mu'allim-i aṣlī*); he had been looking with the truth (*ḥaqq*) for the one who spoke the truth (*muḥiqq*).

[§44] Now that I have come to know that unique person who is the man of the epoch, the Imam of the age, the teacher of the followers of *ta'līm*, the locus of the word (*maẓhar*-i *kalima*), he who enables one to recognize God – praise be to Him – and now that I have surrendered to the fact that he is the [real] instructor, the truthful one, the ruler (*ḥākim*), and I have now that I have surrendered to the fact that he is the [real] instructor, the truthful one, the ruler (*ḥākim*), and I have attained the status of submission, utterly abandoned my own will, and arrived at the realm of learning and subjection, [I realize] that my recognition and knowledge are to be that which my teacher says are [true] recognition and knowledge, and everything else is pure unknowing and ignorance. Proof and demonstration are to be what he says are [correct] proof and demonstration, and everything else is doubt and error. Religion and obedience are to be that which he says are [true] religion and obedience, and everything else is irreligion (*bī-dīnī*), unbelief and innovation (*bid'at*). Whatever comes from him is the straight path, true faith and guidance, and whatever comes from myself, my personal opinion, desire, speculation, intellect, knowledge and insight [and which is contrary to his teachings], is deviation (*ḍalālat*).

[§45] Since the circumstances of this world are [always] changing, if at a certain time or under certain circumstances, the speaker of truth (*muḥiqq*) shows himself to mankind in a different form, expresses himself differently, manifests the truth differently, or institutes the divine law differently [from that of his predecessor], it will not mean that there is any difference in his truthfulness (*muḥiqqī*), because [in his essence] he is free from transformation and alteration (*istiḥāla wa taghayyur*). Transformation and alteration are the necessary attributes of this world, and appear as such in the eyes of the people of this realm.

[§46] If at all [the seeker] were to think that he is independent unto himself because of these changing external circumstances, he has not yet reached the rank implicit in the verse: 'Then they shall find in themselves no impediment touching thy verdict, but shall surrender in full submission' (4:65). Nor will his submission be [true] submission, because he has not yet acknowledged the sovereignty [of the Imam] which is the sovereignty of the absolute ruler (*sulṭa-yi ḥākimī*),

[§47] However, concerning obedience and physical actions, the follower of this way will be always on the watch for the sign and order of the ruler. For his sake the follower will give up his own self, so that he might not desire anything but what he [the Imam] has done, and might not do anything except what he has ordered, for he is the real ruler and disposer. By way of an example, in man the soul is the ruler and administrator of the body; if the soul wishes the hand to move, the hand cannot follow its own will or hesitate, but must obey the soul. If there is a delay in performing that movement, it will be due to some disorder in that person's temper, some disease or illness. Similarly, every craftsman has tools and appliances by means of which he is able to demonstrate his craftsmanship; if they do not work properly, it will be due to some defect or imperfection in them.

[§48] Now man, who is a part of the universe, stands in relation to the command of the administrator and ruler as do the organs and limbs [of the body] in relation to the soul. Indeed, he is in the position of tools and appliances which are at the disposition of the craftsman, to the extent that if he senses even a speck of self-determination, free-will, desire or dislike, any wish to reconsider or interpret the reasons for right and wrong, or to think that things should be like this or that [in contradiction to the command of the instructor], he should realize that it is the result of some imperfection in his essence, some illness in his soul, or some incompleteness in his beliefs. We seek refuge from that in God. When he is cured of such shortcomings and sicknesses, he has reached the degree of the intimate angels who disobey not God in what He commands them (66:6). Indeed, he has left the realm of plurality for the world of oneness, and to the question 'Whose is the kingdom?' he has heard there the answer 'That of God, the one, the omnipotent' (40:16)

[§49] To be brief, once this form [of belief] had taken up its abode within me, much of the curiosity and pursuit of the irrelevant which I had before, when I would run after schools, opinions and confessional bigotry, was cast out ...[43] [And thus] all that resulted from the inconsistency in the attitudes of the followers of the *sharī'at* and the dispute between the exotericists, with its consequences, disappeared, because I realized that all opinions were branches of one root, that all were false, and that all religious doctrines have come from one source (*shakhṣ*) and they were all true in their own time and place: 'Falsehood does not have a beginning, nor will it return' (34:49).

[§50] Despite the fact that in every age some people have remained ignorant of the [real] point and have been covered by a veil, the true religion (*dīn-i ḥaqq*), the straight path (*rāh-i rāst*), which is free from all change, transformation, multiplicity and contradiction, has always been and always will be the one religion and the one path: 'There is no changing the words of God' (10:64). And, in every age, according to the dictate of divine wisdom and the providence of God, a command emanating from God reaches humankind, a command which consists in the promotion of good deeds and a discourse on what is charitable and virtuous. In respect to this, humankind takes up two religious attitudes: one group accepts it and submits to it, whether willingly or unwillingly, and is referred to as, for example, [the followers of] Islam; but another group refuses to accept it, following the practice [of Iblis who said] 'I would never prostrate myself before a man,' (15:33) and show themselves to be rebellious; they are called [the followers of] unbelief (*kufr*). Then the first group [i.e., those who have accepted the revelation] divides into two groups: one who attends to the command (*farmān*), the other who attends to the commander (*farmāndih*, i.e., the Imam). It is in terms of this distinction that the hypocrites are separated from the faithful, the exotericists from the esotericists, the people of legal prescriptions (*sharī'at*) from the people of resurrection (*qiyāmat*), the people of plurality from the people of unity.

[§51] Since all groups are in the realm of opposition (*taqābul*), true constancy (*thubāt-i ḥaqīqī*) necessarily rests with one group which is always with the commander [who is mindful of changing circumstances], while the other groups who, from time to time remain behind with a command, undergo real change (*inqilāb-i ḥaqīqī*). From the point of view of change and degeneration (*qalb wa intikās*), which are necessary attributes of the world of similitude (*kawn-i mushābahat*), relative constancy (*thubāt-i iḍāfī*) is in the form taken by the latter group, who come to a halt with one command and never leave it. [But] the first group, who are attentive to the commander at every moment and obey whatever he prescribes, are necessarily in a state of relative change (*inqilāb-i iḍāfī*).[44]

[§52] In the eyes of the people of opposition and contradiction (*taqābul wa taḍādd*),[45] the world is forever in a state of plurality and contradiction (*munāqaḍat*), alteration and transformation. Thus, the light of certainty can never shine on anyone who stumbles into this desert of bewilderment and confusion, and such a person can never reach the shore of deliverance. He will find nothing but endless wrangling, disputation and tribulation.

[§53] However, in the eyes of the people of gradation (*tarattub*), everything which was, which will be and which now exists, is in its own [proper] time and place, true and tied to the truth; and everything which is not in its [proper] time and place is illusory and severed from the truth. If one sees shortcomings and imperfections, it is the result of imperfections in one's vision; otherwise all the constituent parts of existing things, from the most contemptible to the most noble, are signs and indications, clear testimonies and proofs, in agreement with each other, confirming the truth of each other, and pointing to one meaning: 'We shall show them our signs in the horizons and in themselves, untill it is clear to them that it is the truth' (41:53).

'In everything there is a sign of Him,
proving that He is one.'[46]

[§54] [Finally], in the eyes of the people of unity (*waḥdat*), there is neither this nor that, neither truth nor falsity, neither multiplicity nor oneness, neither resurrection nor religious law, neither outward nor inward, neither origin nor return; everything is He, and apart from Him there exists nothing – nothing in nothing! 'Suffice it not that thy Lord is witness over all things?' (41:53).

[§55] For the first group, truth does not exist and falsity exists; for the second group truth exists and falsity does not; but for the third group [only] the truth exists, and that is all. The knowledge of the first group [is based on] inference from effect to cause, and their obedience is to religious law and tradition (*sunnat*). The knowledge of the second group [is based on deduction from cause to effect, and their obedience is to the resurrection. The knowledge of the third group][47] comes from the one who is knowing (*'ārif*), and their obedience is to know God through God.[48]

In the revelation (*tanzīl*) these three groups are called the 'people of the left,' the 'people of the right' and the 'foremost' (*sābiqān*).[49] The ordinary folk call them [respectively] the 'people of this world,' the 'people of the hereafter' and the 'people of God'. But the elite know them as the 'people of religious law,' the 'people of resurrection' and 'the people of unity'. 'Perfect is the word of thy Lord in truthfulness and justice; no one can change His words; He is the All-hearing, the All-knowing' (6:115).

[§56] From the day I set out on this quest until now when my mind has attained such a form as described, I have, through supplication and prayer, besought from Him, the Lord of majesty, success in adhering to this way and the attainment of the pleasure of my teacher – may God exalt his situation and keep watch over his shadow – in all my words, deeds and thoughts;

and I have sought refuge in my Lord from the whisperings of the devils among the *jinn* and humankind,[50] and from evil concepts, fantasies and imaginings. From Him, I have sought the felicitation of acceptance among the worthy servants.

[§57] Since the majestic court of the sublime presence, the tongue of truth, the perfection of creation – may God exalt his situation – is the point of reference for spiritual guides (*murshidān*) and a haven for those in quest of knowledge (*mustafīdān*), I have delivered a report of my condition, so that I might be favoured with some advice from that source of munificent bounty and infinite compassion, if he should deem it expedient, as to the soundness or error of its formulation, and that he might not deprive me of the honour of his guidance. I wait in hope that this will be granted, so that in the esoteric realm I might contemplate what is pointed out and ponder on what I am instructed; and so that in the exoteric realm I might utter what has been placed on my tongue and do that of which I have been informed; and so that I might refrain from any [contrary] intervention, reasoning or analogy of my own, or with any obedience to opinions and desires attendant on habits of blind imitation, of regulation, or on the demands of traditions, whether true or false, laudable or despicable.

[I also hope that thereby] I might avoid slipping into unbelief and deviation, by guarding myself from mixing what this honoured presence, this holy excellency, has commanded with the conclusions of my own senses, imagination, fantasy, thought and intellect, in so far as this could be possible; and from contaminating what I do, say or think with any taint of hypocrisy or my own [ideas of] what should or should not be done. I only wish, purely for the sake of Him, [the Almighty] most noble, that I might not fall into unbelief and innovation, and that, God willing, I might not be deprived. May I also not remain stuck in my present circumstances, because fear of deprivation is also a characteristic of the failure to submit. Apart from whatever [answer] may be given [to this missive], there neither can be nor will there be any alternative [for me].

[§58] The inconvenience [I have caused] to that august presence has exceeded its bounds, and this humble servant dare not start to apologize. 'But speaking drifts from topic to topic [and] one word leads to another.'[51] Your exalted opinion is more sound in all respects. May the noble shadow prevail, till the extinction of the world, and may the sun of magnificence shine forth from the horizon of perfection. Peace be upon you.[52]

Notes to the Introduction

1. Mentioned in the colophon of the oldest known manuscript of the *Rawḍa-yi taslīm,* copied from the autographed text in 986/1560. It consists of 127 folios, incomplete at the beginning but with additional fragments at the end. The colophon reads: 'These words are written in the noble handwriting of *sulṭān al-du'āt ... wa khwāja-yi kā'ināt* (the king of the *dā'īs* ... and master of creation) ...' For the complete citation, see S. J. Badakhchani, *The Paradise of Submission: A Critical Edition and Study of Rawḍa-yi taslīm* (D. Phil. thesis, Oxford University, 1989), p. 57.

2. The term *sharī'at* (Ar. *sharī'a*), which usually refers to the Islamic religious law, denotes a number of meanings depending on the context. In the *Sayr wa sulūk,* Ṭūsī uses the word variably to mean 'individual legal prescriptions' [§6], 'the science of theology' [§9], 'the religious law' as a whole [§20], as well as the Qur'ānic revelation [§26].

3. See W. Ivanow's introduction to Ṭūsī's *Rawḍat al-taslīm yā taṣawwurāt* (Leiden, 1950), p. xxv.

4. Tāj al-Dīn Shahrastāna, more commonly known as Muḥammad b. 'Abd al-Karīm al-Shahrastānī, the author of *Kitāb al-milal wa al-niḥal* (Book of Religions and Doctrinal Schools), *Kitāb muṣāra'at al-falāsifa* (Book of Wrestling with Philosophers), *Nihāyat al-aqdām fī 'ilm al-kalām* (Ultimate Footsteps in Theology), a Qur'ānic commentary, *Mafātīḥ al-asrār* (Keys to the Secrets), and the famous *Majlis-i maktūb* (Written Sermon). Professor Wilferd F. Madelung, in his article 'Aspects of Ismā'īlī Theology: The Prophetic Chain and the God Beyond Being.' in *Ismā'īlī Contributions to Islamic Culture,* ed. S. H. Nasr (Tehran, 1977), p. 59, says: 'Though widely renowned as an outstanding Ash'arī theologian with an open-minded interest in all religions and philosophies, he was known by some of his contemporaries to incline secretly to Nizārī Ismailism and to spread its message.' Judging from the following evidence, there is little doubt

of Shahrastānī's close association with the Ismailis: (i) his use in the *Majlis* of a vocabulary characteristic of Persian Ismaili texts, such as *ḥukm-i mafrūgh wa musta'nif* (decree of the primordial past and the subsequent future), *'ālam-i khalq wa amr* (realm of creation and command), and *kawn-i taḍādd, tarattub wa waḥdat* (realms of contradiction, gradation and unity); (ii) his sympathetic treatment of the doctrine of *ta'līm* in the *Kitāb al-milal,* where his apparent criticism of the doctrine actually supports it; (iii) his censure of Ibn Sīnā's reliance on intellect alone for the knowledge of God in the *Muṣāra'a;* and (iv) his comments on Ash'arism and indirect support of Ismaili theological viewpoints in the *Nihāyat.* It is worth noting also that Ṭūsī, in his *Muṣāri' al-muṣāri'* (Downfall of the Wrestler), clearly indicates Shahrastānī's association with the Ismaili *da'wat,* and his rebuttal of Shahrastānī's criticism of Ibn Sīnā does not amount to a refutation of the latter's views on the knowledge of God. It is on the basis of such evidence that Ismail K. Poonawala, in his *Biobibliography of Ismā'īlī Literature* (Malibu, Calif., 1977), pp. 254–7, has listed Shahrastānī as an Ismaili author.

5. On Kamāl al-Dīn Ḥāsib there is no reliable report. Afḍal al-Dīn Muḥammad b. Ḥusayn Kāshī or Kāshānī, also known as Bābā Afḍal, is the author of *Anjām-nāma, Jāwdān-nāma,* and eloquent quatrains resembling those of 'Umar Khayyām. His works, which are famous as specimens of Persian prose writing, deal mainly with philosophy, ethics and logic. The Ismaili orientation of some of his writings, especially in relation to the esoteric exegesis of the Qur'ān is evident. According to Jan Rypka, 'Bābā Afḍal,' EI2, vol. 1, pp. 838–9, 'There is no authentic information about his life, and scientific and systematic research into his works has only recently commenced.' See also relevant entries in Dihkhudā's *Lughat-nāma* (Tehran, 1979); Muṣāḥib's *Dā'irat al-ma'ārif-i Fārsī* (Tehran, 1966); and S. Hossein Nasr, 'Afḍal al-Dīn Kāshānī and the Philosophical World of Khwājah Naṣīr al-Dīn Ṭūsī,' in *Islamic Theology and Philosophy: Studies in Honor of George F. Hourani,* ed. M. Marmura (Albany, N.Y., 1984), pp. 249–64.

6. For details on these personalities and Ṭūsī's early education, see Mudarris Raḍawī, *Aḥwāl wa āthār-i Abū Ja'far Muḥammad b. Muḥammad b. Ḥasan al-Ṭūsī* (Tehran, 1975), pp. 5–7, 154–77, and F. J. Ragep, *Naṣīr al-Dīn Ṭūsī's Memoir on Astronomy: al Tadhkira fī 'ilm al-hay'a* (New York, 1993), vol. 1, pp. 16–20.

7. Shihāb al-Dīn's full name, as given by Qāḍī Minhāj-i Sirāj in *Ṭabaqāt-i Nāṣirī,* Eng. tr. H. G. Raverty (New Delhi, 1970), vol. 2, p.

1197, was Abū al-Fatḥ Shihāb Manṣūr. According to Minhāj, he was the governor of the province of Quhistān until 621/1224, and says: 'At that time the Muḥtashim was Shihāb al-Dīn ... I found him a person of infinite learning, with wisdom, science and philosophy in such wise that a philosopher and sage like unto him there was not in the territory of Khurāsān. He used greatly to cherish poor strangers and travellers ...' He further adds that great men of learning, such as Afḍal al-Dīn Bāmyānī and Shams al-Dīn Khusraw Shāh, attended his court. It was Shihāb al-Dīn who persuaded Ṭūsī to write a commentary on Ibn Sīnā's *al-Ishārāt wa al-tanbīhāt.* See Ṭūsī's *Sharḥ al-ishārāt wa al-tanbīhāt* (Tehran, 1377/1957), pp. 2–3, and note 20 below.

8. Apparently Ṭūsī corresponded untiringly with many of his learned contemporaries, and the text of a number of questions and answers arising from his correspondence have survived. See Mudarrisī Zanjānī, *Sargudhasht wa 'aqā'id-i falsafī-yi Khwāja Naṣīr al-Dīn-i Ṭūsī* (Tehran, 1335*s*/1956), pp. 198–221.

9. 'Alā Dhikrihi al-Salām or Li-Dhikrihi al-Salām (lit. 'on his mention be peace') is the honorific title used by Nizārī Ismaili writers for the Imam Ḥasan (d. 561/1166) who enunciated the preaching of the *qiyāmat* (resurrection). His sermons known as the *Fuṣūl-i muqaddas wa mubārak* are quoted frequently in the Alamūt and post-Alamūt Nizārī Ismaili literature. For a number of long quotations from the *Fuṣūl* see Ivanow's edition of Ṭūsī, *Rawḍa-yi taslīm,* pp. 78, 86, 112–17, 126. The main non-Ismaili sources on the Imam Ḥasan are 'Aṭā-Malik Juwaynī, *Tārīkh-i Jahān-gushāy,* ed. M. Qazwīnī (London, 1912–1937), vol. 3, pp. 225–39; Eng. tr. J. A. Boyle, *The History of the World-Conqueror* (Manchester, 1958), vol. 2, pp. 686–97; and Rashīd al-Dīn, *Jāmi' al-tawārīkh: qismat-i Ismā'īlīyān,* ed. M. T. Dānish-pazhūh and M. Mudarrisī Zanjānī (Tehran, 1959), pp. 162–70. See also Marshall G. S. Hodgson, *The Order of Assassins* (The Hague, 1955), pp. 148–59, and Farhad Daftary, *The Ismā'īlīs: Their History and Doctrines* (Cambridge, 1990), pp. 385–92.

10. It was at the request of Nāṣir al-Dīn Muḥtashim (Nāṣir al-Dīn 'Abd al-Raḥīm b. 'Alī) that Ṭūsī composed and translated a number of books, including the *Tawallā wa tabarrā.* Ṭūsī's most important works on ethics, the *Akhlāq-i Nāṣirī* and *Akhlāq-i Muḥtashimī,* are dedicated to Nāṣir al-Dīn .

11. It is probable that this work was designed as a handbook for preachers and teachers of religion. Quoting a Prophetic Tradition, Ṭūsī says: 'If success is companion, then everyday, while investigating

one's situation [i.e. practising what one reads in each chapter of the book], one of the virtues mentioned here will actualize in one's spiritual self, and after forty days he will achieve countless blessings, because "He who purely supplicates to God for forty mornings, the springs of wisdom will flow from his heart to his tongue",' *Akhlāq-i Muḥtashimī,* ed. M. T. Dānish-pazhūh (Tehran, 1339*s*/1960), p. 5. For more details on this book, see Hamid Dabashi, 'Khwājah Naṣīr al-Dīn al-Ṭūsī: The Philosopher/Vizier and the Intellectual Climate of his Time,' in *History of Islamic Philosophy,* ed. S. H. Nasr and O. Leaman (London, 1996), vol. 1, pp. 559–61.

12. An elementary work dealing mainly with esoteric aspects of ethical virtues, the *Gushāyish-nāma,* ed. M. T. Dānish-pazhūh (Tehran, 1341*s*/1962), has an Ismaili overtone but it does not rival the style and mastery of Ṭūsī's later works.

13. Ṭūsī compiled the *Risāla-yi Mu'īniyya,* ed. M. T. Mudarris Raḍawī (Tehran, 1335*s*/1956), in response to a request from Mu'īn al-Dīn, the son of Nāṣir al-Dīn Muḥtashim. The same Mu'īn al-Dīn also requested Ṭūsī to provide a commentary on the book which resulted in the *Dhayl* or *Sharḥ-i Mu'īniyya,* ed. M. T. Dānish-pazhūh (Tehran, 1335*s*/1956).

14. In a supplementary section of the *Akhlāq-i Nāsirī* which he added in the year 663/1264, Ṭūsī remarks: 'In one of the months of the year 663, when some thirty years had passed from the compilation of the book ...,' which confirms that it was compiled in 633/1235. *Akhlāq-i Naṣirī,* ed. M. Mīnuwī and 'A. R. Ḥaydarī (Tehran, 1356*s*/1977), p. 236; Eng. tr. G. M. Wickens, *The Nasirean Ethics* (London, 1964), p. 178.

15. On the *Tawallā* and the *Āghāz,* see the section on 'Ṭūsī's other Ismaili works' in the Introduction.

16. Ṭūsī's alleged correspondence with Ibn 'Alqamī, vizier to the last 'Abbāsid caliph al-Musta'sim, appears to be highly improbable in view of the fact that the vizier was appointed to his office in the year 642/1244, almost a decade after Ṭūsī's arrival in Rūdbār. See Mudarris Raḍawī, *Aḥwāl,* p. 10.

17. 'Alā' al-Dīn Muḥammad succeeded to the Ismaili Imamate at the age of nine in 618/1221, when Chingiz Khan crossed the Oxus river. To combat the Mongols, he appealed to the 'Abbāsid caliph as well as some European powers. With reference to his hospitality and the building of Maymūn Dizh, Shīrīn Bayānī says that 'he was a wise ruler who left for posterity what was best and most exalted.' See her

Dīn wa dawlat dar Īrān-i 'ahd-i Mughul (Tehran, 1367s/1988), pp. 216–17, 230. Ibn al-Fuwaṭī, a Sunni author who served under Ṭūsī as a librarian at the Marāgha Observatory, has also commended 'Alā' al-Dīn on various accounts, in his *Talkhīṣ majma' al-ādāb*, ed. M. Jawād (Damascus, 1962–7), vol. 4, sec. 2, pp. 1081–2.

18. On the *Rawḍa-yi taslīm*, see my comments later in the Introduction. I am in the process of preparing a new edition and English translation of the text.

19. The *Asās al-iqtibās*, ed. M. T. Mudarris Raḍawī (Tehran, 1976) is Ṭūsī's most comprehensive work on logic, written in the same style as Ibn Sīnā's works on the subject.

20. Ibn Sīnā's *al-Ishārāt wa al-tanbīhāt*, ed. S. Dunyā (Cairo, 1960) is one of his most celebrated philosophical works. There are numerous commentaries on the book by known and lesser known authors. Fakhr al-Dīn al-Rāzī's hostile and defamatory commentary attracted the attention of Muḥtashim Shihāb al-Dīn who requested Ṭūsī to comment on the text and provide answers to the criticism. Ṭūsī's work, which he entitled *Ḥall-i mushkilāt al-ishārāt* (Solutions for the Difficulties of the Ishārāt) and is more commonly known as the *Sharḥ al-ishārāt*, re-introduced Ibn Sīnā's *Ishārāt* into scholastic circles, which has since then become a textbook for Islamic philosophy in many universities of the Middle East. For more details see Mudarris Raḍawī, *Aḥwāl*, pp. 433–6.

21. A detailed survey of Ṭūsī's astronomical works appears in Ragep, *Naṣīr al-Dīn Ṭūsī's Memoir*, vol. 1, pp. 20–70.

22. Juwaynī, in his *Jahān-gushāy*, Eng. tr., vol., 2, p. 719, reports as follows: 'Now when I was at the foot of Lammasar, being desirous of inspecting the library, the fame of which had spread throughout the world, I suggested to the King that the valuable books in Alamūt ought not be destroyed ... I went to examine the library, from which I extracted whatever I found in the way of copies of the Koran ... I likewise picked out the astronomical instruments ... As for the remaining books, which related to their heresy and error and were neither founded on tradition nor supported by reason, I burnt them all.'

23. There is no firm evidence to support this accusation made by Sunni writers, apparently to ascribe the destruction of the 'Abbāsid caliphate as a Shi'i conspiracy. It seems that the whole episode, as Juwaynī speaks of it, originated from Hūlagū's suspicion of a number of apocalyptic predictions presented to him by the court astronomer,

Ḥusām al-Dīn Munajjim. Hūlagū solicited Ṭūsī's opinion on the matter and the latter felt compelled to deny his forebodings. See Mudarris Raḍawī, *Yādbud-i haftṣadumīn sāl-i Khwāja Naṣīr al-Dīn Ṭūsī* (Tehran, 1335*s*/1956), pp. 13–14.

24. For an assessment of these views see G. M. Wickens, introduction to his translation of *Akhlāq-i Nāṣirī,* p. 12; also E. G. Browne, *A Literary History of Persia* (Cambridge, 1902–1924), vol. 2, p. 457, and Badakhchani, *Paradise,* pp. 25–6.

25. The Marāgha Observatory gradually became an important centre of learning with a library holding over 400,000 books. Ṭūsī's astronomical tables (*zīj*) compiled in the observatory contained some errors because he was forced to complete his calculations ahead of schedule. For details see Mudarrisī Zanjānī, *Sargudhasht,* pp. 117–20; Mudarris Raḍawī, *Aḥwāl,* pp. 40-56; and Bakhtyār Ḥusain Ṣiddīqī, 'Naṣīr al-Dīn Ṭūsī,' in *A History of Muslim Philosophy,* ed. M. M. Sharif (Wiesbaden, 1963), vol. 1, pp. 565–6.

26. Ṭūsī wrote the *Muṣāri' al-muṣāri'*, ed. Ḥasan al-Mu'izzi (Qumm, 1405/1984) in order to refute Shahrastānī's condemnation of the philosophers in his *Muṣāra'at al-falāsifa,* both texts edited by Ḥ. al-Mu'izzi (Qumm, 1405/1984). In the same work, Ṭūsī is also critical of the Ismaili orientation of the arguments used by Shahrastānī against Ibn Sīnā. See note 4 above.

27. The *Talkhīṣ al-muḥaṣṣal,* ed. 'A. A. Nūrānī (Tehran, 1359*s*/1980) is Ṭūsī's detailed commentary on Fakhr al-Dīn al-Rāzī's book on scholastic theology, *al-Muḥaṣṣal,* or to quote its full title, *Muḥaṣṣal afkār al-mutaqadimīn wa al-muta'akhirīn* (Cairo, 1323/1905). Ṭūsī's work is dedicated to 'Aṭā-Malik Juwaynī.

28. The striking similarities between Ṭūsī's *Risālat al-imāma* (Tehran, 1359s/1980) and the writings of his contemporary Twelver Shi'i theologian, Maytham Baḥrānī, suggest that either the *Risāla* is a modified version of Baḥrānī's chapter on Imamate, or the latter copied the text from Ṭūsī. See Baḥrānī, *Qawā'id al-marām fī 'ilm al-kalām* (Qumm, 1398/1977), pp. 173–92.

29. Regarded as the most important of Ṭūsī's Twelver Shi'i works, the *Tajrīd* has not survived in its original form. Expressions critical of the Ismailis attributed to Ṭūsī are only found in some of the commentaries, of which Ḥasan Ḥillī's *Kashf al-murād: sharḥ-i tajrīd al-i'tiqād,* ed. A. Sha'rānī (Tehran, 1398/1977) is the most popular. Taftāzānī, in the second discourse of his *Sharḥ-i maqāṣid,* denied Ṭūsī's authorship of this work. For details, see 'Abd al-Amīr al-A'ṣam, *al-*

Faylasūf Naṣīr al-Dīn Ṭūsī (Beirut, 1980), pp. 149–55; Mudarrisī Zanjānī, *Sargudhasht*, pp. 182–3; Mudarris Raḍawī, *Aḥwāl*, pp. 422–3.

30. After joining the Mongol court, Ṭūsī changed the exordium of the *Akhlāq-i Nāṣirī* and removed from it references favourable to Ismailism. See Jalāl al-Dīn Humā'ī, 'Muqaddima-yi qadīm-i Akhlāq-i Nāṣirī,' in *Majalla-yi Dānishkada-yi Adabiyyāt-i Dānishgāh-i Tehran*, 3 (1956), pp. 8–9. In fact the changes that Ṭūsī introduced in the text, apart from his omission of the eulogy, hardly amount to ten instances. Words such as *imām* and *muḥiqq* (truthful leader) have been replaced by *sharī'at* and *'ulamā-yi muḥaqqiq* (qualified scholars). Other terms such as *ahl-i ḥaqq* (people of the truth), *nāṭiq* (messenger-prophet) and *asās* (legatee-imam) which are particular to Ismaili texts, are altogether deleted. In spite of these alterations, the Ismaili poet and theologian Fidā'ī Khurāsānī, also known as Ḥājjī Ākhūnd (d. 1342/1923), in his *Hidāyat al-mu'minīn*, ed. A. A. Semenov (Moscow, 1959), p. 112, recognized the *Akhlāq* as an Ismaili text, and says that when Ṭūsī uses the word 'king' he means the Imam 'Alā' al-Dīn Muḥammad. Professor Wilferd F. Madelung has emphasized the Ismaili orientation of the *Nasirean Ethics* in his article 'Naṣīr ad-Dīn Ṭūsī's Ethics Between Philosophy, Shi'ism and Sufism,' in *Ethics in Islam*, ed. R. G. Hovannisian (Malibu, Calif., 1985), pp. 85–101.

31. The *Qawā'id* is printed together with the *Talkhīṣ al-muḥaṣṣal*, pp. 435–68.

32. The *Awṣāf al-ashrāf*, ed. N. Māyil Hārawī (Mashhad, 1361*s*/1982) is the only work that Ṭūsī wrote specifically on the subject of Sufism. Both in the *Akhlāq-i Nāṣirī*, Pers. text, pp. 74–5, and the *Rawḍa-yi taslīm*, Pers. text, pp. 91–2. Ṭūsī is critical of the excesses and malpractices of Sufi disciples. For a discussion of Ṭūsī's views on Sufism, see Madelung, 'Naṣīr al-Dīn Ṭūsī's Ethics,' pp. 85 ff.

33. For Ṭūsī's comments on al-Rāzī's note on the doctrine of *ta'līm*, see the *Talkhīṣ*, p. 43, and for more details, Mudarrisī Zanjānī, *Sargudhasht*, pp. 185–6.

34. Ṭūsī was accompanied on his journey of almost two years by his student, Quṭb al-Dīn Shīrāzī; see Mudarris Raḍawī, *Aḥwāl*, p. 57. According to a letter of the 48th Ismaili Imam, Shāh 'Alī Shāh, Aga Khan II, addressed to Murād Mīrzā of Sidih, the descendents of Ṭūsī were venerated by the local Ismailis in Sidih, a village near Bīrjand, until the late nineteenth century. Ms. dated Rajab, 1300/1882, in the library of The Institute of Ismaili Studies, London.

35. St Augustine, the master theologian of the Latin Church,

was born at Thagaste in North Africa in 354 CE, brought up a Christian, converted to Manichaenism and, after an agonizing inner conflict, was re-baptised in 387 CE. For details, see his *Confessions* (Harmondsworth, 1961).

36. Nāṣir Khusraw, *Dīwān,* ed. M. Mīnuwī and M. Muḥaqqiq (Tehran, 1978), pp. 505–15.

37. In his *al-Munqidh min al-ḍalāl,* Eng. tr. W. M. Watt, *The Faith and Practice of al-Ghazzālī* (London, 1953), pp. 26–7, Ghazzālī states: 'When God by His grace and abundant generosity cured me of this disease, I came to regard the various seekers (after truth) as comprising four groups: (i) The *Theologians* (*mutakallimūn*), who claim that they are the exponents of thought and intellectual speculations; (ii) the *Bāṭinīyah,* who consider that they, as the party of 'authoritative instruction' (*ta'līm*), alone derive truth from an infallible Imam; (iii) the *Philosophers,* who regard themselves as the exponents of logic and demonstration; (iv) the *Sufis* or *Mystics,* who claim that they alone enter into the 'presence' (of God) and possess vision and intuitive understanding.' 'Umar Khayyām, the famous astronomer and poet, enumerates the same groups in his *Risālat al-wujūd,* as quoted in S. Hossein Nasr, *An Introduction to Islamic Cosmological Doctrines* (Rev. ed., London, 1978), p. 20.

38. In Ḥaydar Āmulī's *Jāmi' al-asrār wa manba' al-anwār,* ed. H. Corbin and O. Yahya (Tehran-Paris, 1969), p. 493, and some of the bibliographies, for example Carl Brockelmann, *Geschichte der arabischen Litteratur,* supplement 1 (Leiden, 1937), p. 927, *Sayr wa sulūk* appears as a subtitle for *Awṣāf al-ashrāf.* Since this title does not appear in Ṭūsī's own introduction to the *Awṣāf,* it is possible that at some point the two works appeared in one copy, and subsequently when the *Sayr wa sulūk* was detached from the *Awṣāf* – probably because of its suspect Ismaili authorship and the fact that it was not widely read among the Twelver Shi'is – its title continued to remain with the *Awṣāf.*

39. Ṭūsī's authorship of *Sayr wa sulūk* has been confirmed by Mudarrisī Zanjānī in *Sargudhasht,* p. 195; al-A'ṣam in *al-Faylasūf,* p. 88; Mudarris Raḍawī in *Aḥwāl,* pp. 291–2; and Poonawala in *Biobibliography,* p. 262. On the similarities between *Sayr wa sulūk* and other works of Ṭūsī, compare *Āghāz wa anjām,* p. 43, *Sayr wa sulūk* [§ 39]; *Āghāz,* pp. 19–21, *Sayr* [§ 31–3]; *Āghāz,* p. 7, *Sayr* [§ 48]; *Rawḍa-yi taslīm,* Eng. tr. pp. 143–4, *Sayr* [§ 17]; *Rawḍa,* pp. 126–9, *Sayr,* [§ 28]; *Qawā'id al-'aqā'id,* pp. 458–60, *Sayr* [§ 25–31].

40. Muẓaffar b. Muḥammad [b. Ḥasan] is referred to as Quṭb

al-Dīn in the present text [§ 1], as well as in Ra'īs Ḥasan's *Qaṣīda-yi Ḥasan dar madḥ-i fidāwīyān*, ed. and tr. W. Ivanow, 'An Ismaili Poem in the Praise of Fidawis,' in *Journal of the Bombay Branch of Royal Asiatic Society*, New Series, 14 (1938), pp. 63–7.

41. See Mudarris Raḍawī's introduction to Ṭūsī's *Majmū'a-yi rasā'il* (Tehran, 1335s/1956), p. vi.

42. *Rasā'il Ikhwān al-Ṣafā'* (Beirut, 1957), vol. 4, pp. 195–7. See also 'Ārif Tāmir, *Ḥaqīqat Ikhwān al-Ṣafā'* (Beirut, 1982), pp. 23–4, and Poonawala, *Biobibliography*, p. 20.

43. Al- Sijistānī, *Kitāb al-iftikhār*, ed. M. Ghālib (Beirut, 1980), pp. 52–84.

44. Al-Kirmānī, *Rāḥat al-'aql*, ed. M. Kāmil Ḥusayn and M. Muṣṭafā Ḥilmī (Leiden-Cairo, 1953), pp. 401–38.

45. Al-Mu'ayyad, *al-Majālis*, ed. Ḥ. Ḥamīd al-Dīn (Bombay, 1975–1986), vol. 1, pp. 22–4, 44–8, 72, 450; vol. 2, pp. 121–3.

46. Nāṣir Khusraw, *Zād al-musāfirīn*, ed. M. Badhl al-Raḥmān (Berlin, 1341/1923), pp. 469–84; see also his chapters on the Imamate in *Wajh-i dīn*, ed. G. R. A'wānī (Tehran, 1977), pp. 19–32.

47. On the life, teachings and writings of Ḥasan-i Ṣabbāḥ, see al-Shahrastānī, *Kitāb al-milal*, pp. 203–7; Hodgson, *Order*, pp. 43–5, 127–30; Badakhchani, *Paradise*, pp. 92–101; as well as the following works by Farhad Daftary: *The Ismā'īlīs*, pp. 324–71; *The Assassin Legends: Myths of the Isma'ilis* (London, 1994), pp. 31–44; and 'Ḥasan-i Ṣabbāḥ and the Origins of the Nizārī Isma'ili Movement,' in *Mediaeval Isma'ili History and Thought*, ed. F. Daftary (Cambridge, 1996), pp 181–204.

48. On al-Shahrastānī, see note 4 above. The title *al-Fuṣūl al-arba'a* was probably coined by al-Shahrastānī who renders a summary of Ḥasan's writings. Al-Shahrastāni's view that the arrangement of each chapter is designed to refute a specific sect might also be his own reading of the text. Both Juwaynī and Rashīd al-Dīn have referred tő what al-Shahrastānī calls 'chapters' as 'compulsions' (*ilzām*).

49. Al-Ghazzālī felt obliged to refute Ismaili doctrines on a regular basis. In his *al-Munqidh*, Eng. tr. Watt, p. 52, he says: 'My object at the moment is not to show the falsity of their views, for I have already done so (1) in *Al-Mustaẓhirī*, (2) in *The Demonstration of Truth*, a reply to criticisms made against me in Baghdād, (3) in *The Fundamental Difference (between Islam and Unbelief)*, in twelve chapters, a reply to criticism made against me in Hamadān, (4) in the book of the *Durj* drawn up in tabular form, which deals with feeble criticisms of me

made in Ṭūs, and (5) in *The Just Balance* which is an independent work... .' For more details see Henry Corbin, 'The Ismā'īlī Response to the Polemic of Ghazālī,' in *Ismā'īlī Contributions to Islamic Culture,* pp. 69–98, and Badakhchani, *Paradise,* p. 85.

50. Ṭūsī, *Rawḍa-yi taslīm,* Eng. tr., pp. 147–8.

51. Nāṣir Khusraw says in the Safar-nāma, Eng. tr. W. M. Thackston, Jr., *Nāṣer-e Khosraw's Book of Travels* (*Safarnāma*), (Albany, N.Y., 1986), pp. 91–2: 'So I wrote a note of regret, saying that I would come to him later. I had two reasons for doing this: one was my poverty, and the other was, as I said to myself, that he now imagines that I have some claim to being learned, but when he sees my note he will figure out just what my worth is ... .'

52. For a general discussion of the concept of *amr* in early Ismaili thought, see Paul E. Walker, *Early Philosophical Shiism: The Ismaili Neoplatonism of Abū Ya'qūb al-Sijistānī* (Cambridge, 1993), pp. 14, 25–63.

53. Two-thirds of approximately 140 works attributed to Ṭūsī, among them a number of short treatises, were composed during this period. For more details on Ṭūsī's literary output, see Mudarris Raḍawī, *Aḥwāl,* pp. 333–628; al-A'ṣam, *al-Faylasūf,* pp. 78–95; Mudarrisī Zanjānī, *Sargudhasht,* pp. 161–221; and 'A. Nūrānī's introduction to Ṭūsī's *Talkhīṣ,* pp. xiv–xvii. A tentative chronological list of Ṭūsī's works is given in Badakhchani, *Paradise,* pp. 243–52.

54. See Ṭūsī, *Rawḍa-yi taslīm,* Eng. tr., p. 134, and the colophon of *Sharḥ-al- ishārāt,* vol. 3, p. 420.

55. Juwaynī, *Jahān-gushāy,* vol. 3, pp. 240–1; Rashīd al-Dīn, *Jāmi',* p. 170.

56. Ṭūsī, *Āghāz wa anjām,* ed. I. Afshār (Tehran, 1335*s*/1956), p. 3.

57. Ṣadr al-Dīn Shīrāzī, *Mafātīḥ al-ghayb* (Tehran, 1391/1971), pp. 649–63; Persian tr. M. Khwājawī (Tehran, 1404/1983), pp. 992–1087.

58. Ṭūsī, *Tawallā wa tabarrā* (Tehran, 1339s/1960), p. 565. The Qur'ānic references are 2: 167; 5: 56; 42: 23.

59. On the notions of 'primordial past' and 'subsequent future,' see note 13 to the Translation.

60. Ṭūsī, *Maṭlūb al-mu'minīn,* ed. W. Ivanow, in *Two Early Ismaili Treatises* (Bombay, 1933), pp. 43–55.

61. Ṭūsī, *Rawḍat al-taslīm,* ed. and tr. W. Ivanow (Leiden, 1950).

62. Ṭūsī, *Risāla-yi jabr wa qadar,* in *Majmū'a-yi rasā'il,* ed. M. T.

Mudarris Raḍawī (Tehran, 1335*s*/1956), pp. 8–27. Eng. tr. P. Morewedge, *The Metaphysics of Ṭūsī* (Tehran, 1992), part 2, pp. 1–46.

63. The *Dustūr* appears incorrectly under the authorship of Aḥmad b. Ya'qūb al-Ṭayyibī in *Arba' rasā'il Ismā'īliyya,* ed. 'Ā. Tāmir (Salamiyya, Syria, 1952), pp. 69–101.

64. Ms. in the Library of The Institute of Ismaili Studies, London.

65. For more details on these treatises, see Dānish-pazhūh's introduction to *Akhlāq-i Muḥtashimī,* p. 11.

Notes to the Translation

1. The reference is to the 26th Ismaili Imam, 'Alā' al-Dīn Muḥammad (d. 653/ 1255). See note 17 to the Introduction.

2. The term *thaqalayn* probably refers to mankind (*insān*) and angels (*jinn*), as used in the *Du'ā-yi mubārak-i nudba,* in *Mafātīḥ al-janān,* comp. 'Abbās Qummī (Tehran, 1398/1977), pp. 80–1. Ṭūsī may also be alluding to the well-known Prophetic Tradition of Ghadīr Khumm: 'I leave among you two weighty things, the book of God and my progeny.' Ibn Ḥanbal, *al-Musnad,* ed. M. N. Albānī (Cairo, 1986)), vol. 3, pp. 14–17.

3. On Muẓaffar b. Muḥammad, see note 40 to the Introduction.

4. In his notes to the *Sayr wa sulūk* in the *Majmū'a-yi rasā'il,* p. 115, Mudarris Raḍawī attributes this saying to Anūshīrwān, the Sasanid king of Iran.

5. The lengthy exordium with which Ṭūsī begins the *Sayr wa sulūk* appears to address Muẓaffar b. Muḥammad, but in fact it is in praise of the Imam 'Alā' al-Dīn Muḥammad who appointed Muẓaffar as the chief *dā'ī.*

6. Throughout this treatise and elsewhere in his writings, Ṭūsī refers to himself as 'this humble servant' (*īn banda-yi kamtarīn*), which is a common expression in polite conversation and letter writing in Iran. In the translation, wherever possible, I have replaced this expression with the more convenient pronoun.

7. Ṭūsī refers here to the Ismaili practice of *taqiyya,* precautionary dissimulation of belief in time of persecution, which is sanctioned in the Qur'ān (3: 28) and constitutes a Shi'i principle.

8. An allusion to the Prophetic tradition, 'He who dies without knowing the Imam of his time, dies the death of ignorance,' which is recognized by all schools. See Ibn Ḥanbal, *al-Musnad,* vol. 4, p. 96; al-Kulaynī, *al-Uṣūl min al-kāfī,* ed. M. B. Kamara'ī (Tehran, 1392/1972), vol. 1, p. 342; and al-Qāḍī al-Nu'mān, *Da'ā'im al-Islām,* ed. A. A. A. Fyzee (Cairo, 1383/1963), vol. 1, pp. 25, 27. For variations of this

tradition, see Sami Makarem's introduction to Abū al-Fawāris, *al-Risāla fī al-Imāma* (Delmare, N. Y., 1977), p. 60.

9. The 'respected friend' is most likely Ṣalāḥ al-Dīn Ḥasan [§14], also known as Ḥasan Maḥmūd Kātib. See note 16 below.

10. The term *Mu'ayyad* (lit. 'supported') seems to have been a popular title among the Ismailis, especially in the late Alamūt period. In the *Mu'īniyya,* Ṭūsī addressed Nāṣir al-Dīn Muḥtashim with the similar title of *Mu'ayyad-i muẓaffar,* which led Muḥammad Qazwīnī to conclude that Nāṣir al-Dīn and Muẓaffar b. Mu'ayyad were one and the same person; but Mudarris Raḍawī does not agree with this in his introduction to Ṭūsī's *Majmū'a-yi rasā'il,* p. 120.

11. On al-Shahrastānī, see note 4 to the Introduction..

12. On Afḍal al-Dīn Kāshī and Kamāl al-Dīn Ḥāsib, see note 5 above.

13. *Jamā'at,* literally assembly, congregation or community. In Ismaili literature, from the early Alamūt period, this word is always used for the Ismaili community in particular.

14. Ḥamīd al-Dīn al-Kirmānī makes a similar comment in the *Rāḥat al-'aql,* p. 61: 'It is impossible for the human soul, which is imperfect and in potentiality, to be actualized in the physical world, except through something which is actual in itself, complete in its essence and action. And since, among human beings, no one's soul is actual except those of the Prophets, their legatees and the Imams, and those who have been guided by them ... the actualization [of the soul] is impossible except through them.'

15. On Shihāb al-Dīn, see note 7 to the Introduction.

16. Ṣalāḥ al-Dīn Ḥasan, also known as Ḥasan-i Ṣalāḥ-i Munshī, or as he calls himself in the preface to the *Dīwān-i Qā'imiyyāt,* Ḥasan-i Maḥmūd-i Kātib, was the personal scribe to Shihāb al-Dīn. The *Qā'imiyyāt* is said to be in seven large volumes. I have seen a copy of the first volume, completed in 631/1233, consisting of approximately 150 folios, incomplete at the beginning and at the end. A few of his poems are found in Abū al-Qāsim Kāshānī's *Zubdat al-tawārīkh: bakhsh-i Fāṭimiyān wa Nizāriyān,* ed. M. T. Dānish-pazhūh (2nd ed., Tehran, 1336s /1987), pp. 205–7; and Khayr Khwāh-i Harātī, *Faṣl dar bayān-i shinākht-i imām,* ed. W. Ivanow (3rd ed., Tehran, 1960), pp. 9–10. Mudarris Raḍawī, in his introduction to Ṭūsī's *Majmū'a-yi rasā'il,* pp. 118–19, also cites Mīr Khwānd's *Rawḍat al-ṣafā'* (Tehran, 1339s/1960) and Amīn Aḥmad Rāzī's *Tadhkira-yi haft iqlīm* (Tehran, 1340s/1961) for some of his verses. Ṭūsī acknowledges Ḥasan Maḥmūd's collaboration in the compilation of the *Rawḍa-yi taslīm,* and it is probable

that the series of questions and answers which constitute the 28th 'representation' of the *Rawḍa* was appended to the text by him. For details, see Badakhchani, *Paradise*, pp. 32–3 and 57–9.

17. The word *kūh*, meaning mountain, is a suffix that appears in the names of a number of Ismaili fortresses in Iran. It is difficult to say which of the text editors, Qazwīnī or Taqawī, added the word 'Gird' to specify the place where Ṭūsī met Shihāb al-Dīn. This, however, was a reasonable assumption on their part because Gird Kūh, or Gunbadān Dizh, about 18 kilometers from Dāmghān on the main route between Khurāsān and western Iran, was the site of one of the main Ismaili fortresses. For further information, see Rashīd al-Dīn, *Jāmi'*, p. 117, and Hodgson, *Order*, p. 186.

18. On the Imam Ḥasan 'Alā Dhikrihi al-Salām, see note 9 to the Introduction.

19. On Nāṣir al-Dīn Muḥtashim, see Note 10 to the Introduction.

20. Ṭūsī's deduction is akin to Ḥasan-i Ṣabbāḥ's fourth proposition: 'As the truth is with the first group, therefore, their leader necessarily is the leader of the truthful people.' For details, see al-Shahrastānī, *al-Milal*, pp. 203–7, Hodgson, *Order*, p. 332, and Badakhchani, *Paradise*, pp. 80–109.

21. The 'necessity' alludes to the Qur'ānic assurance of guidance: 'He said, our Lord is He who bestows creation on everything, and further gives [it] guidance' (20: 50).

22. In contrast to acquired knowledge (*'ilm-i iktisābī*), bestowed knowledge (*'ilm-i ladunī*) does not entail the hardship of learning. In the *Rawḍa-yi taslīm*, pp. 39–40, while discussing the types of knowledge, Ṭūsī speaks of bestowed knowledge as divinely-assisted knowledge (*'ilm-i ta'yīdī*). He also states that when someone approaches the universal teacher [i.e., the Imam] with questions concerning recognition (*ma'rifat*), unity (*waḥdat*), etc., and if the teaching is conveyed in exoteric form in an orderly, graduated and relative manner, it is called instructive (*ta'līmī*); but if it consists of esoteric knowledge and is learned instantly, it is called bestowed (*ladunī*).

23. See Ibn Sīnā, *al-Shifā'*, ed. I. Madkūr and A. 'Affīfī (Cairo, 1956), pp. 248–50; and Ṭūsī, *Sharḥ al- ishārāt*, vol. 3, p. 301.

24. Ibn Sīnā, *al-Shifā*, pp. 58–92.

25. For more details, see Ṭūsī, a*l-Risāla fi al-'ilal wa al-ma'l ūlāt*, printed together with *Talkhīṣ al-muḥaṣṣal* (Tehran, 1359*s*/1980), pp. 509–15.

26. This tradition, attributed to the Imam 'Alī b. Abī Ṭālib, asserts his unmediated knowledge of God, as described by Ṭūsī in [§ 20–1]. For similar expressions, see Majlisī, *Biḥār al-anwār* (Tehran, 1956–1972), vol. 3, pp. 270–4.

27. Attributed to the Imam Muḥammad al-Bāqir in Zāhid 'Alī, *Hamārī Ismā'īlī madhhab kī ḥaqīqat aur us kā niẓām* (Hyderabad, 1373/1954), p. 37. The meaning of this tradition is suggested by Ṭūsī in the passage that follows [§ 29].

28. In Shi'i theology, the notion of true faith as a process between 'underestimation' and 'exaggeration' is based on a number of Prophetic Traditions concerning love and hatred for the Imam 'Alī, which are cited in Majlisī's *Biḥār al-anwār*, vol. 39, pp. 246–334. In Ṭūsī's works, this topic is discussed under the heading of 'solidarity and disassociation,' on which see the Introduction, pp. 17–18.

29. Jājarm, now a small town south-east of Bujnurd in Khurāsān.

30. Nāṣir Khusraw makes a similar comment in the *Wajh-i dīn,* p. 127: 'The Imam of the time is the name of God, so is the legatee [i.e. Imam 'Alī] and the Prophet, each in their own time ...' because God is recognized through them. See also Ja'far b. Manṣūr al-Yaman, *Kitāb al-kashf,* ed. R. Strothmann (London, 1952), p. 109.

31. The group Ṭūsī refers to are the Ash'arites who maintained that the divine names (*asma'*) or attributes (*ṣifāt*) are coeternal (*qadīm*) with God.

32. A tradition attributed to the Imam 'Alī in Majlisī, *Biḥār al-anwār,* vol. 3, pp. 13–14, and Rajab al-Bursī, *Mashāriq anwār al-yaqīn*(Tehran, n.d.), p. 112.

33. The second part of this Qur'ānic verse (6:9) has been variously translated as follows: (i) 'And We should certainly have caused them confusion in a matter which they have already covered with confusion' (Yūsuf 'Alī); (ii) 'And [thus] obscured from them [the truth] they [now] obscure' (Pickthall); (iii) 'And thus we would only have confused them in the same way as they are now confusing themselves' (Muḥammad Asad). Although the word *labasa* has various meanings, it is hardly acceptable to assume that God would cause them 'confusion' or 'obscure' the truth from them, but rather, as Asad says in his footnote, 'since it is impossible for man to perceive angels as they really are, the hypothetical angelic message-bearer would have to assume the shape of a human being.' Ṭūsī did not translate this verse into Persian, but the form and context of the expression he uses suggests the reading: 'the manifestation of the command is in the disguise

of a man like any other and dressed before them as they are dressed.'

34. Al-Bursī quotes these words as a Prophetic Tradition in the *Mashāriq,* p. 40. See also Ṭūsī, *Akhlāq-i Muḥtashimī,* p. 20.

35. For details on these three realms in Ismaili literature, see *Haft bāb-i Bābā Sayyidnā,* ed. W. Ivanow, in *Two Early Ismaili Treatises* (Bombay, 1933), pp. 26–7; Khayr Khwāh-i Harātī, *Faṣl dar bayān-i shinākht-i imām,* Pers. text, pp. 30–6; *Rawḍa,* Pers. text, pp. 42–3, 55 and 98–9; as well as Hodgson, *Order,* pp. 173–4.

36. This Prophetic tradition, in its different versions, is a recognized Shi'i tradition. See al-Kulaynī, *al-Uṣūl min al-kāfī,* vol. 1, pp. 332–4, and Khayr Khwāh-i Harātī, *Kalām-i pīr,* ed. and tr. W. Ivanow (Bombay, 1935), pp. 26, 61 and 74.

37. Attributed to the Imam Muḥammad al-Bāqir. See Fayḍ Kāshānī, *Kitāb al-wāfī,* ed. A. Sha'rānī (Tehran, 1375/1955), vol. 1, p. 89, and Muḥammad Riḍa al-Muẓaffar, *'Aqā'id al-imāmiyya* (Cairo, 1391/1971), p. 14.

38. The term *ittiḥād* was amended in Muddaris Raḍawī's edition to *tawḥīd.*

39. The terms 'primordial decree' and 'subsequent decree' are related to the notions of 'primordial past' (*mafrūgh*), i.e., the realm of predestination, and 'subsequent future' (*musta'nif*), i.e. the realm of free will. According to Shi'i theology, mankind dwells between these two realms. What Ṭūsī means in this passage is that a person's spiritual perfection depends on divine grace as well as personal effort. Al-Shahrastānī, in his commentary on the Qur'ān, *Mafātiḥ al-asrār* (Tehran, 1368*s*/1989), pp. 21(b)-23(b), dedicates a full chapter to the explanation of these principles. See also, Ṭūsī, *Rawḍa,* Pers. text, p. 9, and *Risāla-yi jabr wa qadar,* pp. 25–6.

40. Attributed to 'Alī and other Shī'ī Imams, in al-Kulaynī, *al-Uṣūl min al-kāfī,* vol. 3, pp. 3–10.

41. Attributed to the Imam Ja'far al-Ṣādiq. See al-Barqī, *Kitāb al-maḥāsin,* ed. M. Urmawī (Qumm, 1331s/1952), p. 131; al-Kulaynī, *al-Uṣūl min al-kāfī,* vol. 3, pp. 3–9; and Ṭūsī, *Āghāz wa anjām,* p. 7.

42. These lines from the *Fuṣūl-i muqaddas* are cited as a Prophetic tradition by Khayr Khwāh-i Harātī in his *Kalām-i pīr,* Pers. text, pp. 21, 24, 26ff. Similar expressions are found in al-Mu'ayyad fī al-Dīn al-Shīrāzī, *Dīwān,* ed. M. Kāmil Ḥusayn (Cairo, 1949), pp. 72 and 199–210. See also note 8 above.

43. There is a lacuna here in the manuscript, as noted by Mudarris Raḍawī.

44. The distinction that Ṭūsī draws betwen the followers of the 'command' and those of the 'commander' is based on the contrast between the exoteric, incidental and circumstantial aspects of religion which are contingent upon time and place, and the essential, esoteric message which is valid and unchangeable for all times. Whereas the followers of the command conform rigidly to the letter of religious law at all times, the followers of the commander observe the faith in accordance with the guidance of their spiritual leader in every age. It is the former who persistently cling to obsolete and time-bound forms whose faith suffers a real change (*inqilāb-i ḥaqīqī*), whereas the latter who adapt to changing circumstances of time remain faithful to the fundamental tenets of the faith. For more details see Ṭūsī, *Rawḍa,* Pers. text, pp. 64–6.

45. On the threefold division of mankind into peoples of opposition, gradation and unity, see Ṭūsī, *Rawḍa,* Pers. text pp. 76–7, and Hodgson, *Order,* pp. 172–4.

46. Abū al-'Atāhiya, *Diwān* (Damascus, 1965), p. 104.

47. The text has been corrected here by comparing it with Dānishpazhūh's edition of *Guftārī [bandī] az Khwāja-yi Ṭūsī bi rawish-i Bāṭiniyān* (Tehran, 1335s/1956).

48. Probably judging from the manuscript at his disposal, Mudarris Raḍawi reports a lacuna at the end of this sentence, but it is not necessarily demanded by the context.

49. Qur'ān, 9: 100; 56: 10–11.

50. Qur'ān, 114: 4–6.

51. An Arabic proverb. See *al-Munjid* (21st ed., Beirut, 1986), p. 980.

52. In the final passage, Ṭūsī reverts to the formal style of the exordium to address the recipient of his letter directly. See note 5 above.

Bibliography

Abū al-'Atāhiya, Ismā'īl. *Dīwān.* Damascus, 1965.

Abū al-Fawāris Aḥmad b. Ya'qūb. *al-Risāla fī al-imāma,* ed. and tr. S. N. Makarem. Delmar, N.Y., 1977.

Āmulī, Ḥaydar. *Kitāb jāmi' al-asrār wa manba' al-anwār,* ed. H. Corbin and O. Yahya, in *La Philosophie Shi'ite.*Tehran–Paris, 1969.

al-A'ṣam, 'Abd al-Amīr. *al-Faylasūf Naṣīr al-Dīn al-Ṭūsī.* 2nd ed., Beirut, 1980.

Badakhchani, Sayyed Jalal. *The Paradise of Submission: A Critical Edition and Study of Rawḍa-yi taslīm, commonly known as Taṣawwurāt, by Khwāja Naṣīr al-Dīn Ṭūsī.* D. Phil. thesis, Oxford University, 1989.

Baḥrānī, Maytham b. 'Alī. *Qawā'id al-marām fī 'ilm al-kalām.* Qumm, 1398/1977.

al-Barqī, Muḥammad b. Khālid. *Kitāb al-maḥāsin,* ed. M. Urmawī. Qumm, 1331s/1952.

Bayānī, Shīrīn. *Dīn wa dawlat dar Īrān-i 'ahd-i Mughul.* Tehran, 1367s/1988.

Brockelmann, Carl. *Geschichte der arabischen Litteratur.* Weimar, 1898-1902; 2nd ed., Leiden, 1943-1949; *Supplementbände.* Leiden, 1937-1942.

Browne, Edward G. *A Literary History of Persia.* Cambridge, 1902-1924.

al-Bursī, Rajab b. Muḥammad. *Mashāriq al-anwār al-yaqīm fī asrār amīr al-mu'minīn.* Tehran, n.d.

Corbin, Henry.'The Ismā'īlī Response to the Polemic of Ghazālī,' in *Ismā'īlī Contributions to Islamic Culture,* ed. S. H. Nasr. Tehran, 1977, pp. 69-98.

Dabashi, Hamid.'Khwājah Naṣīr al-Dīn al-Ṭūsī: The Philosopher/Vizier and the Intellectual Climate of his Times,' in *History of Islamic Philosophy,* ed. S. H. Nasr and Oliver Leaman. London, 1996, vol. 1, pp. 527-84.

—'The Philosopher/Vizier: Khwāja Naṣīr al-Dīn al-Ṭūsī and the Isma'ilis,' in *Mediaeval Isma'ili History and Thought,* ed. F. Daftary. Cambridge, 1996, pp. 231-45.

Daftary, Farhad. *The Ismā'īlīs: Their History and Doctrines.* Cambridge, 1990.

—*The Assassin Legends: Myths of the Isma'ilis.* London, 1994.

—ed. *Mediaeval Isma'ili History and Thought.* Cambridge, 1996.

Dihkhudā, 'Alī Akbar. *Lughat-nāma.* Tehran, 1979.

Fayḍ Kāshānī, Muḥammad. *Kitāb al-wāfī*, ed. A. Sha'rānī. Tehran, 1375/1955.

Fidā'ī Khurāsānī, Muḥammad b. Zayn al-'Ābidīn. *Hidāyat al-mu'minīn al-ṭālibīn*, ed. A. A. Semenov. Moscow, 1959.

al-Ghazzālī, Muḥammad. *al-Munqidh min al-ḍalāl.* Eng. tr. W. M. Watt, *The Faith and Practice of al-Ghazālī.* London, 1953.

Haft bāb-i Bābā Sayyidnā, ed. W. Ivanow, in *Two Early Ismaili Treatises.* Bombay, 1933, pp. 4-44. Eng. tr. Hodgson, in *The Order of Assassins*, pp. 279–324.

Ḥillī, Ḥasan b. Yūsuf. *Kashf al-murād: sharḥ-i tajrīd al-i'tiqād*, ed. A. Sha'rānī. Tehran, 1398/1977.

Hodgson, Marshall G. S. *The Order of Assassins: The Struggle of the Early Nizārī Ismā'īlīs Against the Islamic World.* The Hague, 1955. Persian tr. F. Badra'ī, *Firqa-yi Ismā'īliyya.* Tabrīz, 1343 s/1964.

Humā'ī, Jalāl al-Dīn. 'Muqaddima-yi qadīm-i akhlāq-i Nāṣirī,' in *Majalla-yi Dānishkada-yi Adabiyyāt-i Dānishgāh-i Tehran*, 3 (1956), pp. 8–9.

—'Ḥikmat-i 'amalī az naẓar-i Khwāja Naṣīr al-Dīn Ṭūsī,' in *Majmū'a-yi sukhanrānīhā-yi 'umūmī-yi Dānishkada-yi Adabiyyāt wa 'Ulūm-i Insānī-yi Dānishgāh-i Tehran.* Tehran, 1969, pp. 37–80.

Ibn al-Fuwaṭī, Kamāl al-Dīn. *Talkhīṣ majma' al-ādāb fī mu'jam al-alqāb*, ed. M. Jawād. Damascus, 1962–1967.

Ibn Ḥanbal, Aḥmad b. Muḥammad. *al-Musnad*, ed. M. N. Albānī. Cairo, 1986.

Ibn Sīnā, Ḥusayn b. 'Abd Allāh. *al-Shifā'*, ed. I. Madkūr and A. 'Affīfī. Cairo, 1956.

—*al-Ishārāt wa al-tanbīhāt*, ed. S. Dunyā. Cairo, 1960.

Ivanow, W.'An Ismaili Poem in Praise of Fidawis,' *Journal of the Bombay Branch of Royal Asiatic Society*, New Series, 14 (1938), pp. 63–72.

Ja'far b. Manṣūr al-Yaman. *Kitāb al-kashf*, ed. R. Strothmann, London, 1952.

Juwaynī, 'Alā' al-Dīn 'Aṭā-Malik. *Tārīkh-i jahān-gushāy*, ed. M. Qazwīnī. London, 1912–1937. Eng. tr. J. A. Boyle, *The History of the World-Conqueror*, Manchester, 1958.

Kāshānī, Abū al-Qāsim. *Zubdat al-tawārīkh: bakhsh-i Fāṭimiyān wa*

Nizāriyān, ed. M. T. Dānish-pazhūh. 2nd. ed., Tehran, 1366 s/1987.
Khayr Khwāh-i Harātī. *Kalām-i pīr*, ed. and tr. W. Ivanow. Bombay, 1935.
—*Faṣl dar bayān-i shinākht-i imām*, ed. W. Ivanow. 3rd ed., Tehran, 1960. Eng. tr. W. Ivanow, *On the Recognition of the Imam*. 2nd. ed., Bombay, 1947.
al-Kirmānī, Ḥamīd al-Dīn. *Rāḥat al-'aql*, ed. M. Kāmil Ḥusayn and M. Ḥilmī. Leiden-Cairo, 1953.
al-Kulaynī, Muḥammad b. Ya'qūb. *al-Uṣūl min al-kāfī*, ed. with Persian tr., M. B. Kamara'ī. Tehran, 1392/1972.
Madelung, Wilferd F. 'Aspects of Ismā'īlī Theology: The Prophetic Chain and the God Beyond Being,' in *Ismā'īlī Contributions to Islamic Culture*, pp. 51–65.
—'Naṣīr ad-Dīn Ṭūsī's Ethics Between Philosophy, Shi'ism and Sufism,' in *Ethics in Islam*, ed. R. G. Hovannisian. Malibu, Calif., 1985, pp. 85-101.
Mafātīḥ al-janān, comp. 'Abbās Qummī. Tehran, 1398/1977.
Majlisī, Muḥammad Bāqir, *Biḥār al-anwār*. Tehran, 1956–1972.
Minhāj-i Sirāj, 'Uthmān b. Sirāj al-Dīn. *Ṭabaqāt-i Nāṣirī*, ed. 'Abd al-Ḥayy Ḥabībī. 2nd ed., Kabul, 1342–1343/1963–1964. Eng. tr. H. G. Raverty. *Ṭabaqat-i Nāṣirī: A General History of the Muhammadan Dynasties of Asia*. New Delhi, 1970.
al-Mu'ayyad fī'l-Dīn al-Shīrāzī, Abu Naṣr Hibat Allāh. *Dīwān*, ed. M. Kāmil Ḥusayn. Cairo, 1949.
—*al-Majālis al-Mu'ayyadiyya*, vols 1 and 2, ed. Ḥ. Ḥamīd al-Dīn. Bombay, 1975-1986; vols 1 and 3, ed. Muṣṭafā Ghālib. Beirut, 1974–1984.
Mudarris Raḍawī, Muḥammad Taqī. *Aḥwāl wa āthār-i Abū Ja'far Muḥammad b. Muḥammad b. Ḥasan al-Ṭūsī*. Tehran, 1354s/1975.
—*Yādbūd-i haftṣadumīn sāl-i Khwāja Naṣīr al-Dīn Ṭūsī*. Tehran, 1335s/1956.
Mudarrisī Zanjānī, Muḥammad. *Sargudhasht wa 'aqā'id-i falsafī-yi Khwāja Naṣīr al-Dīn Ṭūsī*. Tehran, 1335s/1956.
Muṣāḥib, Ghulām Ḥusayn. *Dā'irat al-ma'ārif-i Fārsī*. Tehran, 1966.
Muẓaffar, Muḥammad Riḍā. *'Aqā'id al-imāmiyya*. Cairo, 1391/1971.
Nāṣir Khusraw. *Dīwān*, ed. Naṣr Allāh Taqawī, et al. Tehran, 1304–1307s/1925–1928; ed. M. Mīnuwī and M. Muḥaqqiq. Tehran, 1353s/1978.
—*Safar-nāma*, ed. M. Ghanī Zāda. Berlin, 1341/1922. Eng. tr. W. M.

Thackston, Jr., *Nāṣer-e Khosraw's Book of Travels (Safar nāma).* Albany, N.Y., 1986.
—*Wajh-i dīn,* ed. G. R. A'wānī. Tehran, 1977.
—*Zād al-musāfirīn,* ed. M. Badhl al-Raḥmān. Berlin, 1341/1923.
Nasr, S. Hossein. *An Introduction to Islamic Cosmological Doctrines.* Rev. ed., London, 1978.
—'Afḍal al-Dīn Kāshānī and the Philosophical World of Khwājah Naṣīr al-Dīn Ṭūsī,' in *Islamic Theology and Philosophy: Studies in Honor of George F. Hourani,* ed. M. Marmura. Albany, N. Y., 1984, pp. 249–64.
al-Nu'mān b. Muḥammad, al-Qāḍī Abū Ḥanīfa. *Da'ā'im al-Islām* , ed. A. A. A. Fyzee. Cairo, 1951-61. Partial Eng. tr. A. A. A. Fyzee, *The Book of Faith.* Bombay, 1974.
—*Sharḥ al-akhbār fī faḍā'il al-a'imma al-aṭhar.* Qumm, 1414/1993.
Poonawala, Ismail K. *Biobibliography of Ismā'īlī Literature.* Malibu, Calif., 1977.
Ragep, F. J. *Naṣīr al-Dīn Ṭūsī's Memoir on Astronomy: al-Tadhkira fī 'ilm al-hay'a.* New York, 1993.
Rasā'il Ikhwān al-Ṣafā'. Beirut, 1376/1957.
Rashīd al-Dīn Faḍl Allāh Hamadānī. *Jāmi' al-tawārīkh: qismat-i Ismā'īliyān wa Fāṭimiyān wa Nizāriyān wa dā'īyān wa rafīqān,* ed. M. T. Dānish-pazhūh and M. Mudarrisī Zanjānī. Tehran, 1338s/1959.
Rypka, Jan. 'Bābā Afḍal,' in *Encyclopaedia of Islam.* New ed., London, 1960, vol. 1, pp. 838–9.
Ṣadr al-Dīn Shīrāzī, Muḥammad b. Ibrāhīm. *Mafātīḥ al-ghayb.* Lithograph ed., Tehran, 1391/1971. Persian tr. M. Khwājawī. Tehran, 1404/1983.
al-Shahrastānī, Muḥammad b. 'Abd al-Karīm. *Kitāb al-milal wa al-niḥal,* ed. M. S. Kaylānī. Beirut, 1965. Partial Eng. tr. A. K. Kazi and J. G. Flynn, *Muslim Sects and Divisions.* London, 1984.
—*Kitāb muṣāra'at al-falāsifa,* together with Ṭūsī's *Muṣari' al-muṣāri',* ed. Ḥ al-Mu'izzī. Qumm, 1405/1984, pp. 13–127.
—*Mafātīḥ al-asrār wa maṣābīḥ al-abrār.* Tehran, 1368s/1989.
—*Majlis-i maktūb mun'aqid dar Khwārazm,* ed. M. R. Jalālī Nā'īnī. Tehran, 1350s/1971.
—*Nihāyat al-aqdām fī 'ilm al-kalām.* ed. A. Guillaume. Oxford, 1934.
Sharif, M. M., ed. *A History of Muslim Philosophy,* Wiesbaden, 1963.
Ṣiddīqī, Bakhtyār Ḥusain. 'Naṣīr al-Dīn Ṭūsī,' in *A History of Muslim Philosophy,* vol. 1, pp. 564–80.
al-Sijistānī, Abū Ya'qūb Isḥāq b. Aḥmad. *Kitāb al-iftikhār,* ed. M. Ghālib,

Beirut, 1980.
Tāmir, 'Ārif. *Ḥaqīqat Ikhwān al-ṣafā wa khullān al-wafā'*. Beirut, 1982.
al-Ṭayyibī, Aḥmad b. Ya'qūb. *al-Dustūr wa da'wat al-mu'minīnin li al-ḥuḍūr*, ed. 'Ā. Tāmir, in *Arba' rasā'il Ismā'īliyya*. Salamiyya, Syria, 1952, pp. 69-101.
Ṭūsī, Naṣīr al-Dīn Muḥammad b. Muḥammad. *Āghāz wa anjām* (*Tadhkira*), ed. I. Afshār. Tehran, 1335s/1956.
—*Akhlāq-i Muḥtashimī*, ed. M. T. Dānish-pazhūh. Tehran, 1339s/1960.
—*Akhlāq-i Nāṣirī*, ed. M. Mīnuwī and 'A. R. Ḥaydarī. Tehran, 1356s/1977. Eng. tr. G. M. Wickens, *The Nasirean Ethics*. London, 1964.
—*Asās al-iqtibās*, ed. M. Mudarris Raḍawī. Tehran, 1976.
—*Awṣāf al-ashrāf*, ed. N. Māyil Harawī. Mashhad, 1361s/1982.
—*Guftārī [bandī] az Khwāja-yi Ṭūsī bi rawish-i Bāṭiniyān*, ed. M. T. Dānish-pazhūh. Tehran, 1335s/1956.
—*Gushāyish-nāma*, ed. M. T. Dānish-pazhūh. Tehran, 1341s/1962.
—*Majmū'a-yi rasā'il*, ed. M. T. Mudarris Raḍawī. Tehran, 1335s/1956.
—*Maṭlūb al-mu'minīn*, ed. W. Ivanow, in *Two Early Ismaili Treatises*. Bombay, 1933, pp. 43–55.
—*Muṣāri' al-muṣāri'*, together with al-Shahrastānī's *Kitāb muṣāra'at al-falāsifa*, ed. Ḥ al-Mu'izzī. Qumm, 1405/1984, pp. 3–202.
—*Muqaddima-i qadīm-i Akhlāq-i Nāṣirī*, ed. J. Humā'ī. Tehran, 1335s/1956.
—*Mujārāt-i Ṭūsī*, Ms. in the Library of The Institute of Ismaili Studies, London.
—*Qawā'id al-'aqā'id*, together with *Talkhīṣ al-muḥaṣṣal*, pp. 437–68.
—*Rawḍat al-taslīm yā taṣawwurāt*, ed. and tr. W. Ivanow. Leiden, 1950.
—*al-Risāla fī al-'ilal wa al-ma'lūlāt*, together with *Talkhīṣ al-muḥaṣṣal*, pp. 509–15.
—*Risālat al-imāma*, together with *Talkhīṣ al-muḥaṣṣal*, pp. 424–33.
—*Risāla andar qismat-i mawjūdāt*, in *Majmū'a-yi rasā'il*, pp.57–82. Eng. tr. in P. Morewedge, *The Metaphysics of Ṭūsī* (Tehran–New York, 1992), part 1, pp. 1–53.
—*Risāla-yi ithbāt-i wājib*, in *Majmu'a-yi rasā'il*, pp. 1–14. Eng. tr. in P. Morewedge, part 3, *The Metaphysics of Ṭusī*, pp. 1–14.
—*Risāla-yi jabr wa qadr*, in *Majmū'a-yi rasā'il*, pp. 8–27. Eng. tr. in P. Morewedge, *The Metaphysics of Ṭūsī*, part 2, pp. 1–46.
—*Risāla-yi Mu'īniyya*, ed. M. T. Mudarris Raḍawī. Tehran, 1335s/1956.
—*Sayr wa sulūk*, in *Majmū'a-yi rasā'il*, pp. 36–56.
—*Sharḥ al- ishārāt wa al-tanbīhāt*. Tehran, 1377/1957.
—*Sharḥ-i Mu'īniyya*, ed. M. T. Dānish-pazhūḥ. Tehran, 1335s/1956.

—*al-Tadhkira fī 'ilm al hay'a*, ed. and tr. F. G. Ragep, in his *Naṣīr al-Dīn Ṭūsī's Memoir on Astronomy*, pp. 89–341.

—*Talkhīṣ al-muḥaṣṣal*, ed. 'A. A. Nūrānī. Tehran, 1359s/1980.

—*Tawallā wa tabarrā*, together with *Akhlāq-i Muḥtashimī*, pp. 562–70.

Walker, Paul E. *Early Philosophical Shiism: The Ismaili Neoplatonism of Abū Ya'qūb al-Sijistānī*. Cambridge, 1993.

Yādnāma-yi Khwāja Naṣīr al-Dīn Ṭūsī. Tehran 1336s/1957.

Zāhid 'Alī. *Hamārī Ismā'īlī madhhab kī ḥaqīqat aur us kā niẓām*. Hyderabad, 1373/1954.

Index

سیر و سلوک

سیر و سلوک

از تصنیفات

خواجه نصیرالدین طوسی

ویرایش و ترجمه انگلیسی

از

سیدجلال حسینی بدخشانی

لندن
۱۹۹۸

ربّ اَنعمْتَ فَزِد
رَبَّنَآ آتِنَا مِنْ لَّدُنکَ رَحْمَةً وهیِّئ لَنا مِنْ اَمرِنا رَشَداً

[۱] بزرگترین نعمتی و جسیم ترین موهبتی بر عموم بندگان خداوند زمان و مُحقّ وقت و فرمانده بحق مظهر کلمة اللّه فی العالمین مولی الثقلیَن ملجأ الخافقَین اعلی اللّه کلمته و بسط فی بسیط الارض دعوته، در این روزگار، مخصوص آن ذاتی است که زمام حلّ و عقد و عنان امر ونهی انسان در قبضه‌ی تقدیر و کفّ کفایت عالی قطب الحق والدین اعلم علماء العالم و افضل کُملاء بنی آدم المظفر بن محمد ادام اللّه ظلال جلاله و حرس انوار کماله نهاده اند که برأی جهان آرای کفیل نظم مصالح دو جهانیست و هم بذهن مشکل گشای ترجمان اسرار ربّانی: اذا اراد اللّه تعالی بامة خیراً جعل الملک فی علمائها والعلم فی ملوکها، حقّ جلّ و علا این نعمت مُؤَبّد و مُهنّا گرداناد و همگنان را توفیق شکر کرامت کُناد. انّه اللطیف المجیب.

[۲] مدتی است تا کمترین بندگان محمد الطوسی میخواهد که نموداری از صورت اعتقاد و شمه‌ای از شرح حال خود بر رأی حقیقت نمای مجلس عالی سلطان الدعاة والوزراء دام عالیاً عرضه دارد، تا از آن بارگاه معلّی که منبع افادت اسرار حکمت و مظهر انوار رأفت است تشریف ارشاد و تنبیه بر صواب و خطا و استقامت و انحراف بقدر استعداد این بنده‌ی کمترین ارزانی فرمایند و بآنچه صلاح حال او اقتضا کند دیناً و دُنیاً اشارت رسانند.

[۳] و بسبب آنکه ارادت او چنان بود که این حال در حضور، بَعْد حصول سعادت مثول، پیش مَسند همایون عرضه دارد تا اگر بر سر آن از آن بارگاه جلال افادتی فرمایند از شوائب وسائط جسمانی خالی بُود و بتأثیر و انجاح اولی، [امّا] تفریقی که مقتضای طبیعت روزگار باشد مقتضی تأخیر میشد. و نیز از آ ن روی که

نزدیک عقلاء اخفای هیچ سِرّ واجب تر از سرّ عقیده و مذهب نیست ــ چه خللها [که] از وقوف عوام و جُهّال بر آن مترتب باشد از شرح استغنا دارد ــ نمی خواست که آنرا واسطه ی کتابت در معرض انشاء آرد و خویش را در آن باب از دست دهد تا چون مدت تأخیر از حدّ اعتدال بگذشت و از هجوم اجل که: **اِذَا جَآءَ اَجَلُهُم لا یَسْتَأخِرُوْنَ سَاعَةً وَلاَ یَسْتَقْدِمُوْنَ** اندیشه میکرد، ترسید که مبادا رعایت امثال این نکته ها سبب آفتی کلّی شود و اگر ناگاه عمر بآخر رسد و در مُهمی از مُهمات دینی تقصیری کرده باشد مرگش مرگ جاهلان باشد.

[۴] پس بنیّتی صادق و عزیمتی درست سِرّ ضمیر خود را در صورت کتابت آورد و بر دست مخدوم خود بمجلس ارفع محتشم معظم ناصر الدّولة والدّنیا سلطان الرُّؤَساء فی العالمین افتخار نسب جهان المظفر بن مُؤَیَّد دام رفعته که اشفاق او بر خود و احتیاط در محافظت اسرار مخلصان میدانسته انهاء کرد تا بوقت فرصت بنظر اشرف بگذرانند و آنچه مصلحت دو جهانی بنده‌ی کمترین باشد بفرمایند تا خِطاب: **اِرجِعُوا وَرآءَکُم فالْتَمِسوُا نُوْرَاً** نشنود و از جواب استفاضت مهر انور آن آفتاب کمال محروم نماند. انّهُ وَلِیُّ الاِجابَة.

[۵] و پیش از خوض در مقصود از روی دلیری مقدمه‌ای که ثبت آن مهم میداند ادا می کند و آن اینست که بحکم آنکه در ظاهر سبیل کسانی که در خود مرضی یا المی جسمانی احساس کنند و خواهند که طبیبی که در ازالت انواع امراض و آلام ماهر بود بمعالجه ی ایشان اشارتی کند آن باشد که شرح حال ظاهر خود را از مبدأ احساس آن عارضه تا بآخر پیش آن طبیب بازگویند، تا چون بر اسباب و علامات واقف شود بتدبیر صواب اشارتی کند و از ضّد آن حذر فرماید. در حقیقت نیز شرط کسانی که خواهند که طبیب نفس سِرّ ضمیر ایشان را از اعتقادات فاسده و آلام صور نامطابق که مُؤَدّی بتلف کلی و هلاک جاودانی باشد خلاص دهد هم آن تواند بود که در پیش او شرح حال باطن خود را ــ از مبدأ فکر و تمییز تا نهایت آنکه اعتقادی صورت شده باشد ــ حکایت کند تا بر موضع اصابت رأی و مزال اقدام رتبت تنبیه دهد. پس بنده کمترین اقتدا باین سنت کرد و شطری از مجاری احوال خود را از آنگاه باز که در خود اندک تمییزی احساس کرده است تا اینکه

امروز هست عرضه داشت. و اگر چه اِطنابی که از آن تحاشی مینمود لازم آمد امّا امید از آن منبع کرم و معدن سماحت چنان دارد که در این باب مسامحتی ارزانی فرمایند و بزلّتی که نه بقصد آن اقدام کرده باشد مأخوذ نگردانند. انشاءالله وهو ولیّ الجود و واهب الوجود. و هذا ابتداءُ الخوض فی المقصود.

[۶] چون بحُکم تقدیر و اتفاق ولادت و تربیت بنده ی کمترین در میان کسانی بود که ظاهر شریعت را معتقد و متقلد بودند و اقربا و عشیرات را جز اشتهار بعلوم ظاهر حرفتی و صنعتی نبود، باوّل که در خود تمییزی احساس کرده باستماع اصول و فروع مقاله ی این جماعت نشو و نما یافته بود [و] می پنداشت که بیرون از این شیوه مذهبی و طریقی نتواند بود. اما پدر بنده که مردی جهاندیده بود و سخن اصناف مردم شنیده و تربیت از خال خود که از جمله شاگردان و مستفیدان داعی الدعاة تاج الدین شهرستانه (یافته) بود، در تقلید آن قواعد مبالغه کمتر نمودی، [و] بندهٔی کمترین را بتحصیل فنون علم و استماع سخن ارباب مذاهب و مقالات ترغیب کردی.

[۷] تا اتفاق را شخصی از شاگردان افضل الدین کاشی رحمه الله که او را کمال الدین محمد حاسب گفتنند ی و در انواع حکمت خصوصاً در فنّ ریاضی تقدمی حاصل کرده بود و با پدر بندهٔی کمترین سابقهٔی دوستی و معرفتی داشت بدان دیار افتاد. پدر بنده را باستفادت از او و تردد بخدمت او اشارت کرد و بنده در پیش او بتعّلم فن ریاضی مشغول شد.
و او رحمه الله، بهر وقت در اثناء سخن اهل ظاهر را کسری کردی و مناقضتی که متقلّدان اوضاع شریعت را لازم آید بیان فرمودی و بنده را دلپذیر آمدی. و چون خواستی بغور سخن برسد از آن امتناع نمودی و گفتی آنچه لبّ و خلاصه حقیقت است هنوز با تو گفتنی نیست، که تو کودکی و روزگار ندیده، اگر عمر و توفیق یافتی طلب کن تا بآن برسی. و بهر وقت از روی نصیحت گفتی که ممکن بود که حقّ با کسانی باشد که در نظر این جماعت که تو میبینی حقیر ترین خلق باشند و آیهٔی: **وَ مَا نَرٰىكَ اتَّبَعَكَ إِلاَّ الَّذِينَ هُمْ أَرَاذِلُنَا بَادِیَ الرَّأْیِ** [را] باستشهاد آوردی. پس گفتی که باید بقبح صورت کسی التفات نکنی و اگر

بمَثَل حقّ با بُت پرستان یابی از ایشان بشنوی و قبول کنی.

[۸] القصه بنده‌ی کمترین را در خدمت او معلوم شد که آنچه تا این غایت دیده و شنیده اصلی ندارد، و بدانست که حق بغیر این طایفه هست و در طلب آن جهد باید نمود.
هم در آن نزدیکی خود روزگار چنان اقتضا کرد که او از آن خطّه رحلت نمود و پدر بنده را از این عالم انتقال افتاد. بنده‌ی کمترین در طلب حق و اندیشه تحصیل علمی که مردم را بسعادت آن جهان رساند از خانه‌ی خود هجرت کرد و بحکم وصیّت پدر در هر فن که استادی می یافت استفادت مینمود. اما چون میل ضمیر وشوق نفس بر آن باعث بود که میان حق و باطل از مذاهب مختلفه و آراء متناقضه فرق کند، همت بر تحصیل معقولات مانند کلام و حکمت مقصور داشت.

[۹] اول که در کلام خوضی کرد علم کلام را سراسر بر تصرُّف اوضاع ظاهر شریعت مقرر یافت واهلش را چنان دید که عقل را بر تَمْشیَت مذهبی که از سلف خود تقلید کرده اند اجبار می کنند و بحیلت آنرا حجّتی و دلیلی می انگیزند و محالاتی و مناقضاتی که لازمه آن مذهب باشد عذر می خواهند.
فی الجمله از خوض در آن فن این مقدار فائده گرفت که بر اختلاف مذاهب اندک وقوفی یافت، تا در اثناء آن بدانست که اوّل خلافی که عقلا راست، در معرفت حق و تحصیل کمالی که سعادت آخرت بر آن موقوف باشد ــ بعد از اتفاق بر اثبات حقی و آخرتی بوجهی از وجوه، علی الاجمال لا علی التفصیل ــ آنست که بعقل و نظر مجّرد باین مقصود توان رسید یا با عقل و نظر بتعلیم معلمی صادق حاجت است. پس اهل عالم در این مقام منشعب بدو شعبه‌اند اهل نظر و اهل تعلیم. بعد از آن اهل نظر منشعب می‌شوند باصحاب مذاهب مختلفه چنانکه آن تطویلی دارد، و اهل تعلیم طایفه‌ای‌اند که به اسماعیلیان موسومند و آن اوّل وقوفی بود که بر مذهب جماعت حاصل آمد.

[۱۰] القصه چون از علم کلام جز معرفت احوال ارباب مقالات فائده‌ی دیگر نیافت از آن نفور شد و از استفادت آن علم آهسته ترگشت. بعد از آن در علم

حکمت شروع پیوست. علم حکمت را علمی شریف و بسیار فایده یافت و از فِرَق اهل عالم اصحاب آن علم را خاص دید که عقل را در معرفت حقایق مجالی می دهند و بر تقلید وضعی معیّن اجبار نمی کنند، بل بنای مذهب بر مقتضای عقل می نهند در اکثر احوال ــ الاّ ماشاءَالله. امّا چون سخن بمقصود رسد، یعنی معرفت حقّ جلّ و علا و علم مبدأ و معاد، قواعد ایشان را در آن باب متزلزل دید، چه عقل از احاطه بواهب عقل و مبادی قاصر است و ایشان چون بنظر و عقل خود مغروراند در آن وادی خبط می‌کنند و بر حسب ظنون و خوش آمد سخن می‌گویند و عقل را در معرفت آنچه نه در حدّ اوست استعمال می‌کنند.

[۱۱] بالجمله، در این مطالب دل بر مقالت ایشان قرار نگرفت و حرصی که بر طلب حق بود نقصان نپذیرفت ــ چنانکه در اثناء این کلمات طرْفی از آن یاد کرده آید ــ اما از خوض در حکمت فوائد بسیار حاصل شد، یکی از آن فوائد آن بود که بدانست که هر موجودی که کمالی در او بالقوه باشد، بخودی خود بی‌تاثیر غیر آن کمال از قوه بفعل نتواند آمد. چه اگر ذات او در اخراج آن کمال از قوه بفعل کفایت بودی، کمال خود در تأخیر نماندی، بلکه با وجود ذات حصول آن کمال بافعل مقارن افتادی.
مثالش جسم که در او حرکت بقوه است، اگر غیری در او تأثیر نکند هرگز آن حرکت در او بفعل نیاید، و الاّ همه‌ی اجسام متحرک بودندی. پس چون غیری در آن تاثیر کند آن حرکت که بقوه است بفعل آرد و آن غیر را بآن اعتبار محرّک خوانند و آن جسم را متحرّک گویند.

[۱۲] چون این قضیّه مقرر گشت و نفس را [در] تصدیق بآن ملکه حاصل گشت، بعد از آن نظر بآن نکته افتاد که در علم کلام شنیده بود که خلاف اوّل میان اهل عالم آنست که: معرفت حق بعقل و نظر تنها حاصل آید بی تعلیم معلمی، یا با عقل و نظر بتعلیم حاجت باشد؟ [چون] این قضیه را در آنصورت اعتقاد کرد حقّ با جانب تعلیمیان یافت، چه علم و معرفت خود در مردم بقوه است و مردم سلیم فطرت با وجود عقل و نظر، آنگه این کمال در او از قوه بفعل آیدکه غیری در آن اثری نموده باشد. پس لامحاله خروج این کمال نیز از قوه بفعل بواسطه‌ی تأثیر غیری تواند

بود. و چون آن غیر کمالی فایده دهد که آن کمال علم است بچیزی، فایده دهنده بر قانون گذشته بآن اعتبار معلم باشد و فایده گیرنده متعلم بر قیاس محرّک و متحرّک.
پس معلوم شد که بی‌تعلیم معلمی واکمال مکملی بحق رسیدن ممکن نیست و اهل عالم با کثرت عدد و اختلاف اقوال در این دعوی که بنظر و عقلِ تنها معرفت حاصل می شود بر باطل اند و تعلیمیان بر حقند.

[۱۳] بعد از آن چون این مقدمه روشن شد در تَتَبّع مذهب این جماعت ایستاد، و چون باکسی که بانصاف تقریر این مذهب دادی مُخالطت نداشت و سخن آن جماعت از خصوم ایشان می شنید و می دانست که آنچه خصم از خصم بر حسب خوش آمد خویش بازگوید اعتماد را نشاید، و وقوفی چنانکه می‌بایست نیافت و از اظهار این سِرّ خائف بود.

[۱۴] القصه، روزگاری در این اندیشه بسر برد، پس بحکم آنکه در اثناء این تفحّص بهر وقت از صادر و وارد این ممالک صفت فضائل مخدوم سعید شهاب الدین رضوان الله علیه وخوض او در علوم شنیدی، فرصتی جست و بتوسّط دوستیی که با آن جماعت داشت خدمتی ببارگاه او مشتمل بر دو سه سوال از آنچه در سخن حکماء متناقض یافته و در آن حرف داشت رفع کرد و از جناب او رضوان الله علیه تشریف جواب نامه بخط مخدوم ملک الکتّاب صلاح الدین حسن دام رفعته ارزانی فرمودند و در جواب اسئله گفته: بعذری که جز بمشافهه نتوان گفت ثبتی علمی نمی‌فرمائیم.

[۱۵] بنده بعد از آن فرصتی جسته در سفری که از عراق بخراسان میشد بر محروسه معظمه [گرد] کوه حماه الله تعالی گذری کرد و روزی دو سه خدمت او دریافت و طرْفی از سخن دعوت از لفظ او استماع کرد واو را تعلیق کرده [و] از تقریر او فوائد گرفت. و چون ملازمت خدمت او و مقام نمودن آنجا بسبب موانعی که بذکرش احتیاج نیست مهیا نشد از آنجا بخراسان آمد. بعد از آن بروزی چند، اتفاق را جلدی از فصول مقدس علی ذکره السلام بخطی میانه و کاغذی کهنه در دست

نااهلی که نمی دانست آن چیست مشاهده کرد و آنرا بحیلتی بدست آورد و روز و شب خود را بر مطالعه‌ی آن وقف کرد و از آن کلمات مقدس که نور دلها و چراغ ضمیرهاست بقدر فهم و استعداد ضعیفانه‌ی خود فایده های بینهایت گرفت و اندکی چشم تصّرف باز کرد و دیده‌ی باطن گشوده شد.

[۱۶] پس همّت بر آنکه چون فرصتی یابد خویشتن را میان آن جماعت افکند مقصور گردانید و در آن اوان بحسب باعث ضمیر جهدها نمود تا آن توفیق روزی گردید و بیمن اهتمام مجلس عالی شهنشاهی ناصرالحق والدین اعلاه اللّه و نظر شفقت و تربیت او سعادت اتصال بجماعت و انخراط در سلک مستجیبان دعوت بیافت و حال باینجا رسید که رسید.
هر چند در استماع این فسانه خاطر انور را جز ملال فایده نیست اما بر قضیه‌ی آنچه تقدیم یافت، از حدّت طبیعت و تیمار بنده را، این تقریر مصلحت خود نمود انشاء اللّه تعالی بدامن عفو پوشیده دارند و بسمع رضا اصغا فرمایند. این شرح حال ظاهر است.

[۱۷] و امّا در باطن چون بآن مقام رسید که بدانست حق با تعلیمیان است ـ ببرهانی که تقریر کرده شد ـ بی‌زیادت کلفت تفکّری بدانست که معلم حق، معلم اهل حق تواند بود پس آن معلم که نفوس بتعلیم او از قوه بفعل آید معلم تعلیمیان باشد.

[۱۸] امّا اندیشه‌ی آنکه آن معلم از دیگر معلمان بچه خاصیت ممتاز باشد و چه تعلیم دهد بر خاطر مستولی بُود و بتضرّع از حضرت ربّانی جلّ شانه وضوح و کشف این مطلوب [را] میخواست که اطمینان قلبی حاصل شود. پس با قواعد عقلی که مقرر شده بود و مقدّماتی که از فصول مقدس روشن میشد رجوع می‌کرد و آنرا بیکدیگر تألیف میداد، بعد از آن و از این می‌پرسید و با مبتدیان مجارات و محاورات می‌داشت تا بترتیبی و تدریجی که شرح میدهد صورت اعتقادی که عرضه خواهد شد در ضمیر روشن شد.

[۱۹] اول چنانش نمود که آن معلّم که کمال نفس متعلّم بتوسط او از قوه بفعل آید باید که کامل بالفعل بوده باشد، که هر که کامل بالفعل نبود اکمال دیگری نتواند کرد و اگر آن کمال در او بقوه بوده باشد و بعد از آن بفعل آمده، پس او نیز بمعلّمی دیگر محتاج بوده باشد، یا بتسلسل ادا کند یا انتها بمعلّمی بود که همیشه کامل بالفعل بوده باشد ــ از جهت قطع احتیاج ــ و وجود چنین شخصی را در نوع انسان هم از حکمت و هم از شریعت شواهد [توان] یافت.

[۲۰] اما از حکمت: آنچه حکما گفته‌اند که صاحب قوای قدسیه را هیچ احتیاج به اکتساب نیست، بلکه بمجّرد التفات، نفس او را بی‌واسطه‌ی اکتساب و تجشّم طلب حقایق و معارف بأسرها روشن باشد. و امّا از شریعت: آنچه اهل ظاهر گویند که خداوند علم لدنی را بی واسطه تَعَلُّم همه علوم حاصل شود.
پس دل بر آنکه نوع انسانی از معلّمی که او اول معلّمان باشدد و کامل مطلق بود خالی نیست ــ تا چون بعضی از او بکمال رسدو بعضی نیز بتوسط آن بعض بکمال توانند رسید و افاضت سعادت نخست بترتیبی و بتدریجی که حکمت مبدأ اوّل اقتضا کند دوم نوع را شامل شود ــ قرار گرفت.

[۲۱] و چون ازاین مقام بگذشت و حجابی دیگر از پیش ضمیر برخاست بدانست که چون کمالی که طالب متوجه بآنست معرفت حقّ جّل و علاست که مبدأ موجودات اوست و میان او و میان معلّم اوّل که او را معرفت حق جّل و علا همیشه بالفعل باشد واسطه نتواند بود. چه اگر واسطه فرض شود او اوّل واسطه را شناسد و بتوسط واسطه حق را. پس معرفت حق نیز در او بقوه بوده باشد بتوسط غیری، و چون چنین باشد معلّم اوّل آن غیر باشد نه او، ولیکن ما او را معلّم اوّل فرض کرده ایم پس معلّم اوّل نزدیکترین موجودی باشد بخدای سبحانه و تعالی.

[۲۲] بماند آنکه معرفت او خدای تعالی را بچه وجه تواند بود. چون در این مدت فکری میکرد بخاطر آمد که در علم حکمت در کتاب نفس مقرر شده است که واضح‌ترین معارف و درست ترین تعقّلات معرفت مجرد است بخود خود، زیرا که در این باب استدلال واکتساب را مدخلیتی نیست. و در علم منطق در کتاب برهان

مقرر شده است که علم یقینی مکتسب آنست که از علت معلول را بشناسند و هر چه نه بطریق استدلال از علت برمعلول معلوم کنند یقین مطلق نباشد. و در این مقام چون سخن در معرفت یقینی علت اولیٰ میرود و او را علت نیست، پس با اعتراف حکیم در معرفت علت اولیٰ یقینی نباشد.

[۲۳] و نیز آنجا که حکیم در مراتب موجودات سخن می گوید، نزدیکترین موجودی بعلت اولیٰ عقل اول را می نهد که معلول اول است ولا محاله معرفت او علت اولی راز آنجا تواند بود که او معلول علت اولی است. پس چون او را یقینی نباشد دیگری را طمع یقین در این باب از کجا تواند بود؟ پس اینجا حکیم درِ معرفت خدای تعالی [را] بکلی برخود بسته است و الحق جای حیرت و دهشت هست ــــ و این از جمله مسائلی است که اول گفته آمد که بسبب این مسائل وامثال [آن] این بندهٔ کمترین را دل بر قواعد حکما در معرفت حق قرار نمیگرفت ــ و غرض از ایراد این کلمات اینجا نه بیان عجز حکیم است، بلکه بیان آنست که از تذکر این معانی معلوم شدکه مرتبه معلّم اول نشاید که مرتبه معلول اول بود، بلکه باید درجه او از درجه معلول اوّل بلندتر بود تا معرفت او حقّ جلّ و علا را اشرف معارف باشد.

[۲۴] پس اینجا بتأملی حاجت آمد تا میان معلول اوّل و علت اولیٰ هیچ واسطه تواند بود یا نه؟ ظاهر و مشهور نزد جمهور اهل نظر و خرد آنست که میان معلول اوّل و علت اولیٰ واسطه نیست و مذهب تعلیمیان آنست که صدور موجودات از باریتعالی که مبدأ اوّل است بتوسط چیزیست که آنرا در عبارت متأخرین این جماعت امر او یا کلمه او تعالی میخوانند. وعلت اولیٰ مر عقل کل را که معلول اوّل است امر باری تعالی است، چه باریتعالی از علیّت و معلولیّت منزه است.
و معرفت این نکته و تحقیق حق وابطال باطل در آن از جملهٔ مهمات باشد، چون کسانی که از تحقیق آن غافلند از معرفت حق محجوب مانده اند. الحق در اینصورت هر که از سر انصاف در سخن تأملی کند داند که او را همین حکم بعینه که اصحاب تعلیم بیان کرده اند لازم است از موضعی که او از آن غافل است. [و] بیانش آنست که آنجا که حکیم می‌گوید که از واحد حقیقی جز واحد صادر نتواند شد ــ بجهت آنکه اگر از واحد حقیقی مثلا دو موجود در یک مرتبه صادر شوداعتبار آنکه از او

موجود اول صادر شد غیراعتبار آنست که از او موجود ثانی صادر شد ـــ پس این دو اعتبار متغایر اگر در ماهیت واحد حقیقی داخل باشند، واحد حقیقی نبوده باشد؛ و اگر از او خارج باشند، سخن درصدور ایشان از او هم آن سخن بود در صدور آن دو موجود که فرض کرده‌اند. و چون این دو قسم باطل شد معلوم شد که از واحد حقیقی دو موجود در یکمرتبه با هم صادر نتواند شد، پس معلول اوّل هم واحد است وآن عقل اوّل است.

[۲۵] این تقریر سخن حکیم است و بعد از تقریر این قواعد از آن غافل ماند که بداند که چون از واحد حقیقی واحدی صادرشود بهمه حال باعتباری صادر شده باشد. چه اگر صدور دو موجود اقتضای ثبوت دو اعتبار می‌کند صدور یک موجود اقتضای ثبوت یک اعتبار می‌کند، پس آن اعتبار که باو معلول اوّل از مبدأ اوّل صادر شد آنست که اگر از او قطع نظر کنند هیچ موجودی از او صادر نشود پس هیچ موجود نبود، و درست شد که اثبات این اعتبار حکیم را هم از تمهید قواعد خود لازم آید و از جهت غفلت او از آن راه معرفت حق بر او مسدود گشت.

[۲۶] و معلمی که از آن غافل نبود بحکم آیتی از تنزیل که: **إِنّما اَمرُهُ اِذآ أَرادَ شَيْئاً أَن يَقُولَ لهُ كُن فَيَكُونُ** امر و کلمه نام کرد. چه این آیه اقتضا می کند که صدور موجودات از باریتعالی موقوف بر کلمه‌ی کن است و بلفظ اِنّما که در لغت عربی حصر فایده میدهد بیان کرده که امر هم عبارت از آن کلمه است، پس اثبات این اعتبار را نیز که اهل تعلیم بدعوی ثبوت آن متفرّدند هم از حکمت و هم از شریعت شواهد یافت می شود. اما کسانی که بظاهر این دو طریق متظاهراند از معرفت آن محروم و محجوب مانده اند.

و شک نیست که آن اعتبار یا امر یا کلمه از آنروی که او تعالی باشد چیزی زائد بر ذات مقدّس او نیست و الاّ در ایجاد واحد از آن زائد بتوسطی دیگر احتیاج بودی، و از این طرف که علت معلول است چیزی زائد است پس آن زائد علت معلول [اوّل] است در حقیقت، چه علت و معلول دو امر اضافی اند از جهت آنکه علت نبود تا او را معلولی نبود و معلولی نبود تا او را علتی نبود، و هر چه اضافی بود از حیز تقابُل باشد و تقابُل میان دوچیز تواند بود و دوئی کثرت بُوَد.

[۲۷] پس آنجا که علت و معلولست، از کثرت گزیر نیست و کثرت نشاید مبدأ اوّل موجودات را چه کثرت بی واحد نتواند بود ــ پس چون از این جمله است ــ پس نشاید که مبدأ اوّل حق تعالی اسماؤه از آنجا که مبدأ اوّلست موصوف شود بعلیّت و معلولیّت و وجود و عدم وحدوث و قدم و وجوب و امکان و دیگر اصناف متقابلات و متضّادات و متضایفات، بلکه اعزّ و اعلا از منشأ متقابلین و مبدأ متضادین و مصدر وحدت و کثرت و علت تنزیه و لاتنزیه است و از هر صفت که بر موصوفی اطلاق توان کرد، عدمی یا وجودی، سلبی یا ایجابی، اضافی یا حقیقی، لفظی یا معنوی منزّه واز این تنزیه هم منزّه وَ هَلُمَّ جَرّاً.

[۲۸] و شبهه نیست که این جنس توحید صرف و تنزیه محض جز تعلیمیان را نیست و هیچ کس از اصحاب مذاهب و ارباب ملل او را، جز معلّم این طایفه، حدّ کشف این سِرّ میسر نبوده، چه دیگران سخن از نشاید بود و شاید بود گویند و او از آنجا که: بِکَ عَرَفْتُکَ وَانتَ دَلَّلتَنَی عَلَی نَفْسِکَ. و از اینجا معلوم شد که اطلاق لفظ علت اولیٰ در عبارت حکما بر حق تعالی خطاست و بر امر او سبحانه که مصدر موجوداتست صواب. بلکه هروصف و تنزیه که افاضل حکما و اهل معرفت از عقلاء حواله با علت اولیٰ کرده اند اشاره بامر او سبحانه است که روئی بعالم وحدت محض لایزالی دارد و روئی بعالم کثرت و امکان. و او از آنجا که اوست از هردو روی منّزه و متّعالی است. چنانکه در عبارت پیشوای محقّان لذکر هم السلام آمده است: ما جاءَ فی اللّه فهو فینا امّا مردِ مرد باید که اینجا در غلو یا تقصیر نیفتد. چه مَزالّ اقدام بسیار است و صراط مستقیم، دین اللّه بین المقصر والغالی، از موی باریکتر است و از شمشیر تیز تر.

[۲۹] و در این موضع حکایتی از حال گذشته بخاطر بندهٔ کمترین آمد، هر چند سخن دراز می شود، اما بحکم عذری که در مقدمه تمهید کرده است ایراد می‌کند تا ارشادی که در آن باب لازم باشد ارزانی فرمایند انشاءَاللّه.

در آنوقت که هنوز بجماعت نه پیوسته بود و بر مذهب حق زیاده وقوفی نیافته، به جاجرم با فقیهی مجاراتی افتاد، در اثنأ آن سخن فقیه اسماعیلیان را کسری کرد، سبب پرسیدم، گفت ایشان امام را خدا دانند چه لفظ مولینا که بزعم ایشان جز خدا

را گفتن روا نیست بر امام اطلاق می‌کنند. گاه می‌گویند مولینا علی (ع) و مولینا محمد (ص) و گاه اللّهم مولینا و امثال آن می‌گویند و می‌نویسند و آنچه بدعا از خدا باید خواست از مولینا می‌خواهند. بنده گفت اگر بنظر انصاف نگری چون قاعده‌ی مذهب ایشانست که خدا را جز به امام نمیتوان شناخت پس بنا براین قاعده نسبت امام بخدا از روی دلالت او بر خدا چون نسبت اسم باشد بمسمّیٰ. نه عادت اهل عرف آنست که یک لفظ را بر اسم و مُسمّیٰ اطلاق می‌کنند — زید را زید گویند و نام ملفوظ یا مکتوب او را هم زید گویند — تا از این جهت قومی را خیال افتاده است که اسم و مسمّیٰ یکی است. پس اگر اسماعلیان نام خدا را بر آنکس که دلیل باشد بر خدا اطلاق کنند از قاعده اهل لغت و عادت [اهل] عرف عدول ننموده باشند و ایشان را باین سبب غلو لازم نیاید و شناعتی بر ایشان متوجه نشود. آن فقیه این سخن را جواب نداشت انصاف بداد، چه این عذر ایشان را بجای خویش است و بسر سخن بنده آمد.

[۳۰] برحسب فحوای این قواعد مرتبه‌ئی بالای مراتب معلولات روشن شد و آن مرتبه‌ی امر است که اوّل علل و مبدأ مراتب است و بوجهی متوسط میان خالق و خلایق و بوجهی منتهی درجات و معاد کاینات و آخر موجودات است و معرفت امر اوّل حق سبحانه، از آنجا که اوست، یعنی از روی وحدت معرفت خدا بخدا بود در حد معرفت: **شَهِدَ اَللّٰهُ اَنَهُ لآ إِلَهَ إلاَّهُوَ** اشرف درجات یقین واکمل وجوه معارف. نه چون معرفت از معلول علت را که این معرفتی یقینی نیست. چه حقیقت معرفت چنانکه گفته اند این است: ما عرفناک حق معرفتک. **وَ مَا قَدَرُوا اللّٰهَ حَقّ قَدْرِهِ.**

[۳۱] و در علوم حقیقی محسوس شده است که ورای عالم محسوس عالمی دیگر هست معقول که نسبت آن عالم باین عالم چون نسبت جان باشد با تن، و از اینجاست که آنرا عالم روحانی می گویند و این عالم را جسمانی و بازاءِ هر محسوسی در این عالم معقولی در آن عالم است و مقابل هر شخصی اینجا روحی آنجا و نظیر هر ظاهری اینجا باطنی آنجا، و همچنین بازاءِ هر معقولی آنجا محسوسی اینجا و مقابل هر روحی آنجا شخصی اینجا، و نظیر هر باطنی آنجا ظاهری اینجا که آن معقول مصدر این محسوس باشد و این محسوس مظهر آن معقول.

مثلاً اینجا اگرمحسوسی نماید که آنجا بازای او معقولی نبود، آن نمایش باطل بود و مانند سراب و صورتهائی باشد که مبرسمان و اصحاب مالخولیا بینند. چه هیچ فرع بی‌اصل نتواند بود و اگر آنجا معقولی فرض کنند که بازاء آن اینجا محسوسی نباشد، آن معقول و همی یا خیالی تواند بود که آنرا هیچ حقیقتی نبود چه هیچ موجودی معطل نیست. و در عبارت تنزیل شهادت و غیبت وخلق و امر آمده یعنی دو عالم روحانی و جسمانی.

[۳۲] پس اگر کلمه‌ی باری تعالی را ــ که قیام موجودات در عالم و وصول هر یکی بکمال خویش از او و باوست ــ بعالم محسوس تعلقی نبودی، عالم محسوس اصلاً موجود نبودی و چون تعلقی هست و آن تعلق هم از این جنس تواند بود پس از روی حس هم محسوس باشد. پس امر و کلمه را در این عالم لامحاله ظهوری باشد و مظهر او شخصی بود از اشخاص مردم که بنظر ظاهر مانند دیگر اشخاص محسوس برآید و ببالد و پیر شود و بتعاقب یکی بجای دیگری بنشینند تا آن قیام محفوظ ومستدام بود: **وَلَوْ جَعَلْنٰهُ مَلَکاً لَجَعلنٰهُ رَجُلاً وَ للَبَسْنا عَلَیهِمْ ما یَلْبِسُونَ.**
و در عالم روحانی مجرّد عالمی باشد بعلمی نا مُتناهی و قادر بقدرتی نامُتناهی و جملگی علوم و کمالات از او بر عقول و نفوس فائض: کنّا اظلة عن یمین العرش فسبحناه فسبحه الملائکة و آن ذات امر یا کلمه‌ی باری تعالی باشد که مرتبه‌ی او از مراتب ممکنات و معلولات عالیتر است و جملگی ممکنات و معلولات مطیع و مسخر فرمان اویند: **إِنْ کُلُّ مَن فِی السَّمٰوٰتِ وَ الأَرْضِ إِلَّآءَاتِی اَلرَّحْمٰنِ عَبْدَاً** و از آنجا که اوست از هر دو عالم متعالی و از وحدت و کثرت و مشابهت و مباینت و حقیقت و اضافت مبّرا و منزّه است. **سُبْحٰنَ رَبِّکَ رَبِّ الْعِزَّةِ عَمَّا یَصِفُونَ** تا کمالی که در هر دو کون در نفوس و اشخاص کائنات بقوه باشد بواسطه نور تعلیم و اضائت هدایت او از قوه بفعل آید. **اَلَّذِی أَعْطَیٰ کُلَّ شَیءٍ خَلْقَهُ ثُمَّ هَدَیٰ** و چون باول صدور موجودات از امر بود و باو [به] کمال میرسد، مبداء او بوده باشد و معاد با او، و اول او بود و آخر هم او، و دایره‌ی وجود باو بهم رسد: **هُوَ اَلاوّلُ وَ الآخِرُ وَ الظّٰـهِرُ وَ الباطِنُ وَ هُوَ بِکُلِّ شَیءٍ عَلیمٌ.**

[۳۳] پس باین وجه او را سه اعتبار لازم آید، اعتباری آنکه [او] شخصی مانند دیگر اشخاص است. و اعتباری آنکه او علّت است و دیگران معلول و او معلّم

ودیگران متعلم و او کامل و دیگران ناقص. و اعتباری دیگر آنکه او خود اوست و هیچ چیز را جز او استحقاق اطلاق اسم سببِ وجود نه. و صورت چنانست که از سه کون که در عبارت اهل دعوت میآید، کون مشابهت و کون مباینت و کون وحدت، از این سه اعتبار مذکور است.

[۳۴] و دلیل آنکه نوع انسان بظهور او از دیگر انواع بسایط و مرکّبات عالم محسوس ممتاز است از روی حکمت آنست که انسان اشرف کائناتست، چه از موالید ثلاثه او شریفتر است. و موالید ثلاثه از عناصر و ارکان شریفتراند. و عناصر و ارکان از مبادی جسمانی خویش یعنی هیولی و صورت شریفتراند. پس شریفترین مصادر هم در شریفترین مظاهر ظهور کرده.

[۳۵] و از روی شریعت و ظاهر تنزیل، آن امانت که آسمانها و زمینها و کوهها از قبول آن عاجز بودند و نوع انسان آنرا قبول کرد که: **إِنَّا عَرَضْنَا الْأَمَانَةَ عَلَى السَّمٰوٰاتِ وَ الْأَرْضِ وَ الْجِبَالِ فَأَبَيْنَ أَنْ يَحْمِلْنَهَا وَ أَشْفَقْنَ مِنْهَا وَ حَمَلَهَا الْإِنسٰنُ إِنَّهُ كَانَ ظَلُوماً جَهُولاً** بعد از قبول آن امانت استحقاق بسجود ملائکه‌ی مقرّبین که اشرف مخلوقاتند او را ثابت گشت **وَ إِذْ قُلْنَا لِلْمَلٰئِكَةِ اسْجُدُوا لِأٰدَمَ فَسَجَدُوٓا إِلَّآ إِبْلِيسَ** نزول ظهور شخص معرفت باری در اشخاص نوع انسانی بظهور او در میان ایشان از دیگر انواع کائنات گواهی دادند و هر آینه چون ظهور او در این عالم بسبب آنکه او کمال این عالم است، تا این عالم باقی باشد از او خالی نتواند بود که: لَوْ خَلَتِ الارضُ مِن امامٍ ساعةً لَمادَت بِاهلها.

[۳۶] و همچنین واجب باشد که خلق را با نوار هدایت او راه باشد و الاّ از رسیدن بکمال باز مانند و فایده ظهور باطل شود. و چون در کون مشابهت علاقه که لازم اشخاص انسانی است به قیام شخصی بعد شخصی معلوم تواند شد چه اگر از آن علاقه که دلیل بود بر اتصال و تعاقب قطع نظر کنند، طریق وصول خلق باو مسدود گردد. و علاقه دو نوع تواند بود روحانی و جسمانی. روحانی نصّ یکی باشد بر دیگری و جسمانی اتصال مولود بود بوالد بر سبیل تعاقب، تا باین دو علاقه اتصال آن اشخاص بیکدیگر معلوم شود و اثر: **وَ جَعَلَهَا كَلِمَةً بَاقِيَةً فِي**

عَقِبِهِ و حکم: **ذُرِّيَّةً بَعْضُهاَ مِن بَعضٍ** روشن گردد و عموم اهل عالم را باستشهاد آن دو دلیل یعنی ولادت و نصّ بشخصی که مظهر آن نور باشد راه بود.

[۳۷] هر چند خواصّ را نشانی دیگر باشد، که آن اثری بود از آثار عالم وحدت، و آن تفرد او بود بدعوی آنکه خدای را به خدا میشناسم و خلق را بخدا میرسانم. که هیچ کس را جز او این دعوی و دعوت مسلم نتواند بود. تا از هر سه کون شواهد بر وحدت لایزال او دلالت کرده باشد و حجت خدای بر خلق تمام شود: **قُلْ فَلِلّهِ اَلْحُجَةُ اَلبٰلِغَةُ.** پس باین مقدّمات و قضایا مرتبه معلم اول و خاصیتی که او بدان ممتاز است، تا او کامل مطلق باشد و دیگران ناقص و بتکمیل او محتاج روشن شد.

[۳۸] بماندْ آنکه او چه تعلیم دهد و خلق چه گونه از تعلیم او بکمال رسند؟ در این مقام بعد از تدّبر و تفکّر بسیار و مراجعه بمطالعه کلام بزرگواران آنچه صواب ضمیر بندهٔ کمترین شد این است که عرضه خواهد شد:
اولاً بحکم آنکه حکماء بیان کرده‌اند که بوسیله استدلال از معلول بعلت، یقین محض حاصل نمیتواند شد. و منتهای درجات اهل نظر آنست که بمعلول علت را شناسند، پس هیچ کس از اهل نظر خدا شناس نتواند بود. و نیز چون معرفت بقول اهل نظر مثال و صورتی است که از معروف در ذات عارف حاصل آید و هر مثال و صورت که در ذات عارف حاصل آید غیر معروف بود پس معرفت عارف صورت موهوم خویش را بوده باشد در حقیقت، نه معروف را، و از این جهت فرموده اند: کلّ ما میّز تموه باوهامکم فیٰ ادق معانیه مصروف عنه مردود الیکم مصنوع و مخلوق مثلکم و چون عبادت بر معرفت موقوف است، و حال معرفت اینست، حال عبادت چگونه باشد**إِنَّكُمْ وَ مَا تَعْبُدُنَ مِن دُونِ اللّهِ حَصَبُ جَهَنَّمَ أَنتُمْ لَهَا وٰرِدُونَ** اینست نهایت اهل نظر در طلب کمال.

[۳۹] و امّا اهل تعلیم را قاعده آنست که هر کس در هر درجه‌ای که باشد بمعرفت معلم خود عارف، و معلم او بمعرفت معلم خویش، تا آنجا که بمعلم اوّل رسد و او خدا را بخدا شناخته باشد. پس او نیز خدا را بخدا شناخته باشد.

در فصول مقدس آمده که همه را بمعرفت من عارف باید بودن، که شخص بمعرفت من عارف و بتوحید من موحد، تا حقیقت معرفت و اتّحاد و وحدت بکلی موجود و تحقیق العباده مشهود. و شاهد این حکم در شریعت و ظاهر تنزیل نصّ قرآن است که:**أُولَٰئِكَ الَّذِينَ هَدَى اللَّهُ فَبِهُدَاهُمُ اقْتَدِهْ** و آنکه بمجرد اقرار بکلمه‌ی لا اله الاالله در کون شریعت حکم به خداشناسی نمیکنند تا اقرار بمحمد رسول الله بآن مضاف نمیشود.

[۴۰] از روی حکمت و اعتبار عقلی، چون هر دو عالم ظاهر و باطن بیکدیگر مربوطند، آنچه آنجا بعین است اینجا بأثر است و از احوال این عالم بر احوال آن عالم استدلال توان گرفت. پس چون درین عالم تأمل میرود، بقای ماده بصورتست، چون هیچ ماده بی صورت نتوان بود، و تکثر و اختلاف ماده هم بسبب تکثر و اختلاف صورتست. چه موادّ در حقیقت و ماهّیت با یکدیگر مشارکند. و هر گاه اختلاف از این صور مرتفع شود با یکدیگر متحد شوند. مثلاً آب صورت آبی دارد و هوا صورت هوائی، میان ایشان مخالفت و تکثّر باشد، امّا اگر آب از صورت آبی منسلخ شود و صورت هوائی پذیرد و با هوا متحد شود، میان ایشان مباینت نماند.
در آنعالم نیز، نفوس باختلاف مراتب، از آنروی که از یک مبدأ فائض شده اند بماهیت مُشارکند و بقای ایشان با قتباس صورتی است که سبب آمدن ایشان باین عالم است. پس اگر صورتی که در نفس متعلم مُمثل بود همان صورت باشد که در نفس معلّم او ممثل باشد، و آن چنان بود که بمعرفت معلم عارف بُود — چرا که او با معاد خود بر استقامت باشد — پس میان نفس او و نفس معلم مباینت و تکثر نماند، و چون حجاب مرتفع شود، متعلم به معلم رسد و بوحدت او متحد گردد. پس بمعاد خود رسیده باشد.
و اگر آن صورت مخالف این صورت باشد، چنانکه [در] اقتباس صورت، نفس متعلم متابعت رای و هوای خود کند یا تقلید کسی که متابعت رای و هوای خود کرده باشد، در ظلمات برزخ بماند و بحجاب کثرت که ظل هستی است محجوب شود. **كَلَّا إِنَّهُمْ عَنْ رَبِّهِمْ يَوْمَئِذٍ لَمَحْجُوبُونَ.**

[۴۱] امّا چنانکه هر که در این عالم طالب چیزیست، تا اوّل سرمایه ندارد هم

از جنس مطلوب، و بعد از آن جهد نکند در تحصیل مطلوب، بمطلوب نرسد. مثالش دهقان تا تخم نپاشد و زراعت نکند، بَر برنگیرد، و بازرگان را تا اصل مال نبُود و تجارت نکند، سود نیابد. و صیاد تا خَرخَسه بدست نیاورد و طلب صید نکند، صید را در دام نیاورد. و علیٰهذا، در این عالم نیز تاطالب کمال عطیّتی نیابد که از حکم مفروغ که بجای سرمایه است بازرگان را، و آن نفس پاک و دل صافی است که **إلاَّ مَنْ أَتَی اللّهَ بِقَلْبٍ سَلِیمٍ** و اکتسابی از حکم مستأنف که بجای تجارتست بازرگان را، و آن تسلیمی است از سر بصیرت: **وَ مَن یُسْلِمْ وَجْهَهُ إِلَی اللّهِ وَ هُوَ مُحْسِنٌ فَقَدِ اسْتَمْسَکَ بِالعُرْوَةِ الوُثْقیٰ** تا بازدواج هر دو بیکدیگر و باستغراق مستأنف در مفروغ بدرجه کمال: **لَهُمْ دَارُالسّلٰمِ عِندَ رّبِهِمْ وَ هُوَ وَلّیُهُم** نرسد. اینجا مایه از جنس سود است. آنجا نزول مؤمن از نور حق آفریده اند: خلق المؤمن من نوراللّه و المعرفة نور یقذفه اللّه فی القلب چه اگر بمبدأ خلق المؤمن من نور اللّه نبودی، بمعاد فاذا امر به الحق عرفه نرسیدی، که معاد عود الشئ الی ما بدأ منه است.

[۴۲] علی الجمله و التفصیل، باین مقدمات و شواهد عقلی و شرعی معلوم و مقرر شد که نهایت مسالک اقدام طالبان راه حق آنست که توفیق یابند تا معلّم خود را بشناسند و بمعرفت او عارف شوند چنآنکه در فصول مقدس میفرماید که خدا شناسی امام شناسی است.

[۴۳] و چون بندهٔ کمترین باین مقام رسید، بدانست که حاصل کار و منتهی طلب تسلیمی است که لازم مذهب اهل تعلیم است: **فَلاَ وَرَبّکَ لاَ یُؤْمِنُونَ حَتّیٰ یُحَکِّمُوکَ فِیما شَجَرَ بَیْنَهُمْ ثُمَّ لاَ یَجِدُوا فِی أَنفُسِهِمْ حَرَجاً مِّمّا قَضَیْتَ وَ یُسَلِّمُوا تَسْلِیماً** چه سالک را تا اینجا که در مقام تحکّم بود، فکری و اندیشه‌ای و نظری که باستدلال عقلی معلم اصلی را طلب کند میکرد و بحقّ مُحقّ را می‌جُست.

[۴۴] پس چون [آن] یگانه را که مرد وقت و امام زمان و معلم تعلیمیان و مظهر کلمه و شخص معّرف خدای سبحانه است بشناخت و بمعلمی و مُحقی و حاکمی او اقرار داد و بمقام تسلیم رسید، و اختیار بکل الوجوه از دست او برفت، و در کون متعلمی و محکومی آمده، معرفت و علم او آن باشد که معلم او گوید، معرفت

و علم است، و هر چه جز آن جهل و نادانی محض. و حجت و برهان آن باشد که او گوید، حجت و برهان است و هر چه جز آن شبهه و غلط. و دین و طاعت آن باشد که او گوید، دین و طاعت است، و هر چه جز آن بی دینی و کفر و بدعت. و هر چه از او آمده است، راه راست و ایمان و هدایت، و هر چه از خود و رأی و هوی و نظر و عقل و دانش و بینش خود گوید ضلالت باشد.

[۴۵] و چون در این عالم احوال گردنده است، اگر در وقتی یا حالی محقّ خود را در صورتی دیگر بخلق نماید یا بیانی دیگر فرماید یا حقی دیگر ظاهر کند یا شریعتی دیگر نهد، در محقی او هیچ تفاوت صورت نبندد، که او از استحاله و تغیُّر منزه است. این استحاله و تغیر از لوازم این عالم است و بنظر اهل این کون چنان نماید.

[۴۶] و اگر هیچ گونه، بسبب تبدیل این احوال ظاهر در خود تصرّفی احساس کند هنوز بدرجه: **ثُمّ لایَجِدُوا فِی أَنْفُسِهِم حَرَجاً ممّا قَضَیْتَ وَ یُسَلِّمُوا تَسْلیماً** نرسیده باشد و تسلیمش نه تسلیم باشد، بلکه هنوز بحکومت او اقرار نکرده باشد که تصرف حاکمی است نه محکومی. این در باب معرفت است.

[۴۷] و اما در باب طاعت و اعمال جوارح. صاحب این راه پیوسته منتظر اشاره و فرمان حاکم باشد، و خودی خود را در راه او فراغ دهد تا چون حاکم و مدّبر حقیقی اوست، جز آنکه او کرده باشد نخواسته باشد و جز آنکه او فرموده نکند. مثلا، در مردم نفس که حاکم و مدبر بر بدنست، اگر آن نفس خواهد که بدست حرکتی کند، دست را در آن حرکت جز طاعت نفس هیچ اختیاری و تردّدی نباشد و اگر تاخیری در اقتضاء آن حرکت افتد بسبب خللی بود که در مزاج آنکس[یا] مرضی و آفتی است که بدست او رسیده باشد. و همچنین هر صانعی را آلاتی وادواتی بود که بواسطه آن اظهار صنعت خود کند و اگر آن آلت چنانکه باید بکار نتوان داشت، سبب آفت و نقصانی بود که راجع بآلات وادوات بود.

[۴۸] و همچنین مردم که جزوی از عالم است که بر فرمان مدّبر و حاکم

بمنزلت جوارح و اعضاء بود در طاعت نفس، بل بمثابت آلات وادوات در تصرف صانع، بحدّی که اگر مثقال ذرّه‌ای از خویش تصرفی و اختیاری و خواستی و نخواستی و معاودت نظری یا معرفت وجه صلاح و فسادی یا اندیشه‌ی شاید و نشایدی احساس کند آنرا مقتضای نقصان ذات و بیماری نفس و ناتمامی اعتقاد خود داند، نعوذ بالله منه. و چون از این عیوب و آفات سلامت یافته باشد، بدرجه‌ی فرشتگان مقرّب رسیده باشد: **لا یَعْصُونَ اللّهَ مَآ امَرَهُم** بل از کون کثرت بیرون آمده باشد و در عالم وحدت خطاب: **لِمَنِ المُلْکُ [الیوم]** را، جواب: **لِلّٰهِ الواحِدِ القَهّار** شنیده.

[۴۹] القصه بنده‌ی کمترین را چون این صورت در ضمیر متمکن شد، بسیاری از فضولی و طلب مالا یعنی که پیش از این داشت از تتبع مذاهب و مقالات و تعصّب در امر دیانات از سر بیرون شده... از مناقضت احوال اصحاب شریعت و منازعت اهل ظاهر با یکدیگر و چیزی که بدان سبب میبافت بکلی زایل گشت. چون بدانست که همه مقالات از یک اصل منشعب شده است و همه باطل و مذاهب از یک شخص ظاهر شده و همه بجای خویش و بوقت خویش حق بوده **وَمَا یُبْدِئُ الْبٰطِلُ وَمَا یُعِیدُ.**

[۵۰] الاّ آنکه در هر روزگاری قومی از نکته‌ای غافل مانده اند و بحجابی محجوب شده. دین حق و راه راست که از تغیّر و استحالت و تکثر و مناقضت منزه است همیشه یک دین و یک راه بوده است و خواهد بود: **لاَ تَبْدِیلَ لِکَلِمٰتِ اللّٰهِ.** اما در هر وقت چنانکه حکمت الهی و عنایت ایزدی اقتضا میکند، فرمانی مشتمل بر مصالح اعمال و خطابی متضمن خیرات و حسنات اضافی از حق بخلق میرسد و خلق در آن دو مذهب گیرند. قومی آنرا قبول کنند و طوعاً او کرهاً منقاد شوند و رقم اسلام بمثل بر ایشان کشند. و قومی از آن ابا کنند و بر سنت: **لَمْ اکُنْ لاَسْجُدَ لِبَشَرٍ** تمرد اظهار و برقم کفر موسوم شوند. بعد از آن طایفه اول بدو شعبه منشعب شوند، گروهی را نظر بر فرمان باشد و گروهی را نظر بر فرمانده. پس بدین امتیاز اهل نفاق از اهل ایمان و اهل ظاهر از اهل باطن و اهل شریعت از اهل قیامت و اهل کثرت از اهل وحدت جدا باشند.

[۵۱] پس آنجا که همگان در عالم تقابل اند ثبات حقیقی لازم یک طایفه بود که همیشه با فرمانده باشند و انقلاب حقیقی با دیگر طوایف که یک چندی بفرمان دیگر باز مانند. از جهت قلب و انتکاسی که لازم کون مشابهت است ثبات اضافی صورت حال این قوم باشد که بفرمانی باز ایستند و از آن در نگذرند و انقلاب اضافی لازم آن قوم اول که بلحظه بلحظه مترصد فرمانده باشند و بهر چه ایشان راباز دارد ایستند.

[۵۲] پس در نظر اهل تقابل و تضاد عالم سراسر کثرت و مناقضت و تغیّر و استحالت است. چنانکه هر که در این تیه حیرت و ضلالت افتد هرگز نور یقین بر او نتابد و بساحل خلاص نرسد و جز قیل و قال و خصومت و وبال حاصل نیابد.

[۵۳] و در نظر اهل ترتّب در جهان آنچه بود و آنچه آید و آنچه هستی یابد، هر چیز بجای خویش و بوقت خویش حقّ است و با حقّ بسته. و هر چه نه بوقت خویش ونه بجای خویش باطل است و از حق گسسته. عیب و نقصان دیدن از سبب نقصانیست که درباصره‌ی بصیرت بیننده است و اِلاّ همگی اجزاءِ موجودات از اخس گرفته تا باشرف رسیده آیات و دلالات و حجج و بیّنات اند و با یکدیگر موافق و یکدیگر را مصدّق و بر یک معنی دال: **سَنُرِيهِمْ ءَايٰتِنَا فِى الأَفَاقِ وَ فِىٓ أَنْفُسِهِمْ حَتّىٰ يَتَبَيَّنَ لَهُمْ أَنَّهُ الْحَقُّ**

وَ فِیْ کُلِّ شَیْءٍ له آیة تَدُلُّ عَلَی انّهُ واحِدُ

[۵۴] و در نظر اهل وحدت این و آن و حق و باطل و کثرت وحدت و قیامت و شریعت و ظاهر و باطن و مبدأ و معاد نیست، همه اوست و جز او هیچ و هیچ در هیچ: **أَوَلَمْ يَكفِ بِرَبِّكَ أَنَّهُ عَلَىٰ كُلِّ شَىْءٍ شَهِيدٌ.**

[۵۵] نزدیک طایفه اوّل حق نیست و باطل هست و نزدیک طایفه دوّم حق هست و باطل نیست و نزدیک طایفه سوّم حق هست و بس. معرفت طایفه‌ی اول استدلال از معلول بر علت و طاعتشان شریعت و سنت، معرفت طایفه‌ی دوم

[استدلال از علت بر معلول و طاعتشان متابعت قیامت و معرفت طایفه‌ی سوم] عارف بودن بمعرفت کسی که عارف بود و طاعتشان خدا را بخدا دانستن.
و در تنزیل این سه قوم را اهل شمال و اهل یمین و سابقان می خوانند و در عبارت عوام اهل دنیا و اهل آخرت و اهل خدا و در عرف خاص اهل شریعت و اهل قیامت و اهل وحدت: **وَ تَمَّتْ کَلِمَتُ رَبِّکَ صِدْقاً وَ عَدْلاً لاَّ مُبَدِّلَ لِکَلِمٰتِهِ وَ هُوَ السَّمِیعُ العَلِیمُ.**

[۵۶] حال بنده‌ی کمترین از آنروز که پای در راه طلب نهاده است تا اکنون که ضمیر را صورتی بر این صفت که حکایت کرده حاصل آمده بتضرع و ابتهال از حضرت ذوالجلال توفیق ملازمت این طریقه و تحصیل رضای معلّم خود اعلی الله امره و حرس ظِلاَلَهُ، در اقوال و افعال و افکار میخواهد و از وسواس شیاطین جن و انس و افهام و اوهام و خیالات فاسده پناه بخداوند خویش می برد. و سعادت انخراط در سلک بندگان شایسته از او می طلبد.

[۵۷] و چون بارگاه جلال مجلس عالی لسان الحقیقه مکمل الخلیقه اعلی الله امره مرجع مرشدان و ملاذ مستفیدانست، انباء این حال بتقدیم رسانید تا از آنجا که کرم فیاض و عواطف نامتناهی باشد اگر صلاح دانند بانعام اعلامی از صواب و خطا این صورت مثال دهند و از تشریف تنبیه محروم نگردانند.
امید مساعدت توفیق میدارد که در باطن آن تصّور کند که بدان اشارت فرمایند و آن اندیشد که بیادش دهند و بظاهر آن گوید که بر زبانش نهند، و آن کند که بدانش دارند و از خود بهیچ تصّرف و نظر و قیاس و متابعت رأی و هوای ملازمت عادت تقلید وضع و اقتضای سنت گذشته، خواه حق و خواه باطل، خواه محمود، خواه مذموم راضی نشود.
و مقتضیات حسّ و خیال و وهم و فکر و عقل خود به قدرت و حِسبت استطاعت بآنچه از آن حضرت بزرگوار و جناب مقدس فرمایند بر نیامیزد تا در کفر وضلالت نیفتد. و آنچه کند و گوید و اندیشد بهیچ شایبه از ریا و بایست و نبایست خود ملوث نکند. بل خالصا لوجهه الکریم خواهد تا در شرک و بدعت نیفتد. و انشاءَالله محروم نگردد و در این مقام نیز موقوف نماند که خوف از حرمان هم از سجیه‌ی قصور تسلیم باشد. بآنچه آید جز چنان نباید و نشاید.

[۵۸] تصدیع آن جناب از حد گذشت و بنده‌ی کمترین را یارای تمهید معذرت نتواند بود اما **الحدیث ذوشجون والکلام یجُرالکلام** رأی عالی در همه ابواب صائب تر و سایه بزرگوار تا منقرض عالم پاینده و آفتاب اجلال از افق کمال تابنده **والسلام**.

Naṣīr al-Dīn Ṭūsī

SAYR wa SULŪK